HOW TO GET TO THE WILDERNESS
WITHOUT A CAR

A directory for public transportation and wilderness recreation opportunities in the western United States, including Alaska, and western Canada.

"The main thesis of this book is that you don't need a car to reach many of the national parks, wilderness areas and other unspoiled lands scattered across the western United States and Canada . . ."

from the preface of
the book by Lee Cooper

PUBLIC TRANSPORTATION TO WILDERNESS

In the western United States, including Alaska, and western Canada

LEE W. COOPER

DEAN JACOBSON, ILLUSTRATOR

First edition 1982, Second edition, 1985

Library of Congress Number: 81-90339
International Standard Book Number: 0-9607116-1-9

Lee Cooper and Frosty Peak Books, Publishers
PO Box 80584, Fairbanks, Alaska 99708/PO Box 4073,
Malibu, California 90265

FREE UPDATES

In January of each calendar year after 1985, until
further notice, send a business-size stamped, self-
addressed envelope to: Lee Cooper, Box 4073, Malibu,
CA 90265, to obtain a listing of changes in transportation
services in the previous year. Outside of the U.S.A.,
send a self-addressed envelope and an international
money order or cheque payable through a U.S. bank in
the amount of two (2) U.S. dollars.

Every effort has been made to insure that the information
in this book is correct as of the time of publication.
If you are aware of inaccuracies or changes that should
be made, please write to me at the above address and
I will get the word out.

Lee Cooper
Fairbanks, Alaska
Spring, 1985

PREFACE

The main thesis of this book is that you don't need a · car to reach many of the national parks, wilderness areas, and other unspoiled lands scattered across the western United States and Canada.

There is probably not a trail guide published in North America that does not contain some driving directions and yet few make any mention of public transportation. It is ironic that self-propelled wilderness activities such as hiking, crosscountry skiing, and snowshoeing seem to require a private automobile to reach the trailhead. Ours is a car conscious society, and yet private automobiles have been heavily indicted as a source of air pollution, they are the main components of a transportation system dependent on fossil fuels, and lives are taken daily in traffic accidents. Many people have chosen not to own a car, for these reasons, and for economic ones. Many other people who own a car have chosen not to use them except where alternative transportation does not exist or is impractical. This book is a directory of opportunity for these people and for others interested in visiting unspoiled land and also anxious to decrease their dependence on private automobiles.

ACKNOWLEDGMENTS

My thanks to friends with whom I lived in Seattle and Fairbanks while I was writing this book, to the many readers of the first edition who provided constructive criticism, and to my parents, Leon and Alberta Cooper, for their help and encouragement. And also, thanks to the many people who accompanied me on trips to areas included within this book and to the transportation companies and administrative agencies who freely provided me with additional information.

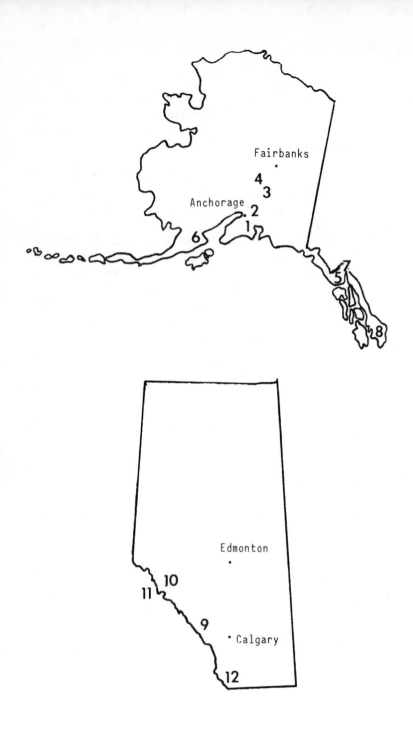

Fairbanks
4
3
Anchorage
2
1
6
7
5
8

Edmonton

10
11
9
Calgary
12

TABLE OF CONTENTS

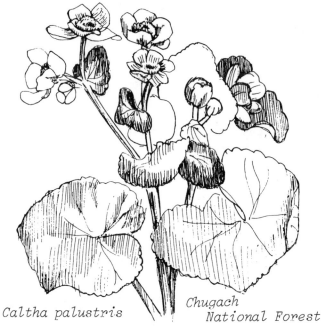

Caltha palustris

*Chugach
National Forest*

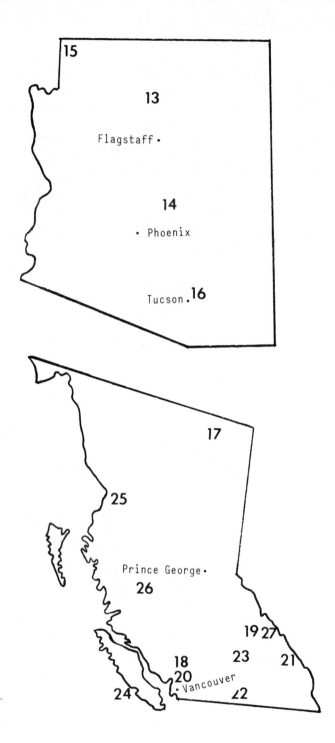

TABLE OF CONTENTS

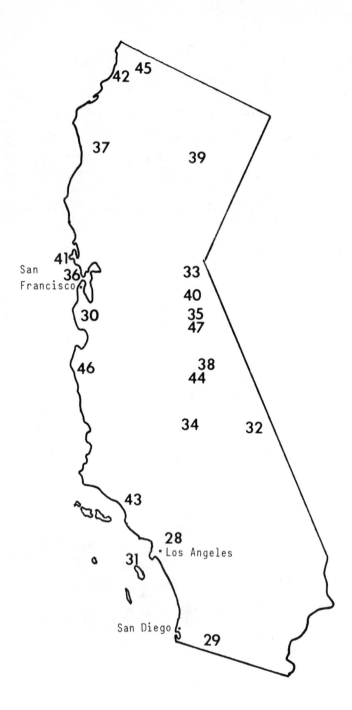

42 45

37

39

San
Francisco

41
36

33

40

35
47

30

46

38
44

34

32

43

28
Los Angeles

31

San Diego

29

TABLE OF CONTENTS

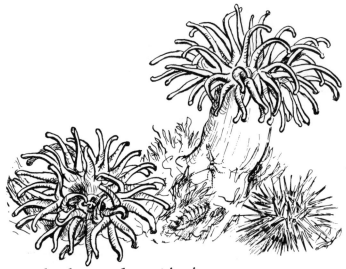

Anthopleura elegantissima
Golden Gate National Recreation Area

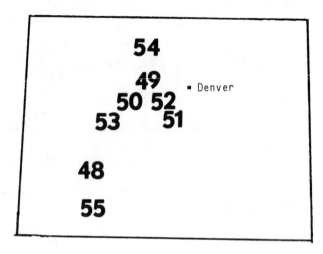

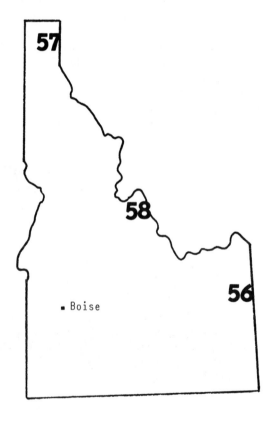

TABLE OF CONTENTS

Myosotis alpestris
Palisades Backcountry Management Area

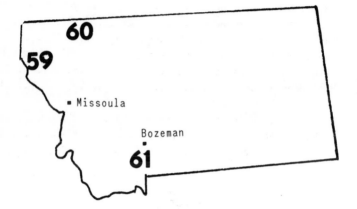

60

59

■ Missoula

Bozeman

61

■ Sante Fe

Albuquerque■ **63**

62

TABLE OF CONTENTS

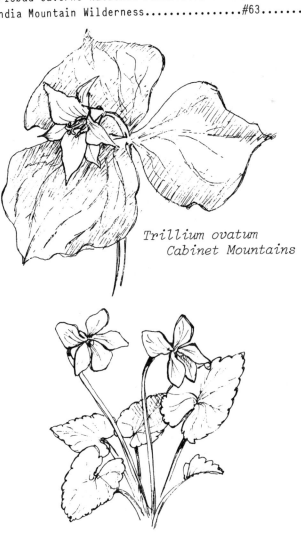

Trillium ovatum
Cabinet Mountains

Viola spp.
Sandia Mountain Wilderness

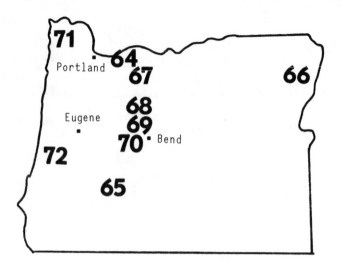

71
Portland
64
67
66

68
Eugene
69
70 Bend

72

65

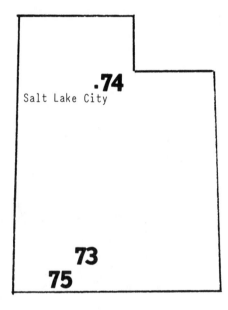

.74
Salt Lake City

73
75

TABLE OF CONTENTS

Lone Peak, Utah

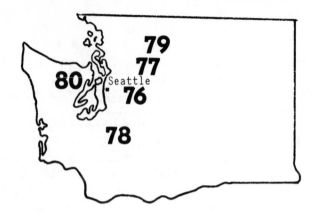

79
77
80 Seattle
76
78

83
82
Cody
81
Jackson

Rock Springs

TABLE OF CONTENTS

Geranium maculatum

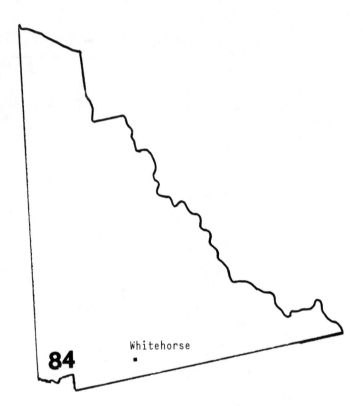

Whitehorse

84

TABLE OF CONTENTS

Zion National Park

INTRODUCTION

I have tried to inventory most of the major wilderness areas, national parks and national forests in the western United States and Canada for public transportation access combined with backpacking, crosscountry skiing and snowshoeing opportunities. Of course a wilderness experience is a state of mind and the reader should not feel limited to the blocks of land covered in this directory. A city park or a quiet country road can offer the same insights that inspired Joseph Wood Krutch and Henry David Thoreau. Nevertheless, for practical reasons, I chose to limit my inventory to areas where there are substantial opportunities for travel away from motorized traffic. In all cases, these areas offer opportunities for overnight camping.

Public transportation is undeniably less convenient than the private auto and in many cases you will need to walk a certain distance from the train or bus station before reaching the actual trailhead. In most cases, I have set an arbitrary limit of three miles or five kilometers, the distance an average person walks in an hour, as the maximum distance from a transit stop. (Incidently, in describing distances in this book, I have adhered to the prevailing measurement system used in each country covered; miles or feet in the United States and kilometers (km) or meters (m) in Canada.) I have used designated stops for this three mile criterium. On many smaller buslines, drivers will let you off and pick you up at places that may be closer to the trailhead, but are not official bus stops. If you are willing to walk more than three miles on roads before really getting started, or consider hitchhiking an acceptable mode of transportation, the number of wilderness areas that can be reached will increase over the number documented in this book.

Another inconvenience for public transportation users is obtaining the necessary permit to travel in a specific wilderness area. Many areas, because of overcrowding, have limits on entry and in a few cases it is not possible to obtain the permit by mail. The issuing ranger station is likely to be inconvenient at best to reach using public transportation. In this worst possible scenario, a call or letter to the authorities will probably elicit a more flexible response. In all cases, using public transportation requires more planning, not only to make advance contact with park or forest personnel, but also to schedule bus connections optimally. It should be obvious that it is to your advantage to have all of your food and equipment with you as you approach the primitive area; you won't have the flexibility to drive twenty miles to a supermarket.

It is recommended that contact be made with the company providing transportation to an area to determine fares and schedules. I have deliberately left out specific fares and schedules because these can become quickly out of date. The transportation companies providing service are listed in each area entry. Phone numbers and addresses of each company are listed in alphabetical order in Appendix I. In some respects it may have been convenient to list addresses and phone numbers within each area description, but since many transit companies serve several areas within the book, I decided to cut back the unnecessary duplication and place all of the addresses and phone numbers in one place.

The administrative offices for the specific wilderness or park can also be contacted and these phone numbers and addresses are arranged alphabetically in Appendix II. Most can provide you with free or inexpensive maps, brochures and general information on the area you will be visiting for the trouble it takes you to write a card.

This book is not designed to serve as a trail guide, but rather a supplementary directory of opportunity for public transportation access. I have listed some of the useful trail guides for the areas covered in Appendix III. Since many trail guides are not widely distributed, I have included in Appendix IV the addresses of the publishers of the guides listed. Some larger publishers do not care to deal with individual orders, but many trail guide publishers are on the cottage industry level and welcome your business. I have also included in this appendix the addresses of several bookstores or services that specialize in selling outdoor travel books of many publishers by mail.

In Appendix V are listed the addresses of state and provincial tourism authorities. These government funded agencies will send free information, maps and brochures to anyone who requests it. Be as specific as possible, telling them what you are interested in seeing and that you will be using public transportation.

OTHER RESOURCES

The Official Airline Guide (2000 Clearwater Drive, Oak Brook, IL 60521) is subscribed to by travel agents and larger libraries. It contains flight schedules worldwide for all major airlines. It is difficult at first to fathom all of the codes used, but once mastered, the twice monthly published directory can tell you which airlines are flying which routes and it can give you a range of their airfares.

Russell's Official National Motor Coach Guide (8 3 4 Third Avenue SE, PO Box 278, Cedar Rapids, IA 52406) does the same thing for buses, publishing timetables monthly for Greyhound, Trailways and a number of other bus companies. It is not as readily found in libraries as is the Official Airline Guide, but a suggestion to your librarian might improve your access to intercity bus information.

There are also train timetables published, but both AMTRAK and VIA Rail (addresses in Appendix I) will send you their current national schedules free on request.

Airlines often advertise special fares in metropolitan newspapers. Don't neglect the financial pages; business travelers are the bread and butter of airline industry profits and airlines advertise amidst the stock market listings to attract them. The travel section of the Sunday paper is also used occasionally, although offerings for package tours to American style resorts in third world countries are more common. The third page of the New York Times Sunday Travel section has a useful column called "The Practical Traveler." The Los Angeles Times (also subscribed to by many libraries) has a comprehensive Sunday travel section that often has information for independent travelers.

A WORD ABOUT FARES

Public transportation can be cheaper than using a private automobile, particularly when car depreciation, insurance and other expenses are considered. It is possible to save even more depending on the form of public transportation used. Greyhound and Trailways have relatively inexpensive fares on a per mile basis and they also have passes that allow unlimited riding for a week to several months. Airfares can be cheaper than point to point bus transportation, particularly on certain high volume, competitive routes such as New York-San Francisco and Chicago-Los Angeles. Savings of up to 40% off the regular coach fare can be obtained by buying "supersaver" tickets. Rules vary with each airline, but generally the ticket must be round-trip, purchased a week to a month in advance and you must stay at least a week (in some cases, just a Saturday night), but less than sixty days. A plethora of other discounts may be available, including family fares and "no-strings" discount fares on a new route

for an airline. Because of airline deregulation in the
United States, there are no hard and fast rules governing
airfares. Canadian airfares are no less confusing with
charters and youth discounts possible. It is to your
advantage to find a good travel agent who is informed
on fare structures for the city that you plan to fly
to. If in doubt, call the airlines serving the route
to find out all the possible discounts and their accompany-
ing restrictions.

AMTRAK fares are relatively simple by comparison. There
are regular fares based on a per mile basis. Sleeping
car accomodations are additional. One free stopover is
allowed enroute for each one way ticket purchased. Discounts
are possible by purchasing round trip excursion tickets
which do not permit stopovers. Family groups also receive
discounts and AMTRAK has in the past loosely defined
what constitutes a family. If you are traveling as a
couple, but are unmarried, buy your tickets using one
last name and you can save money. AMTRAK has also had
unlimited mileage tickets available outside of the peak
travel seasons. These allow travel over one of three
sections of the country or throughout the country for
an additional charge. AMTRAK fares are generally more
expensive than motorcoach fares for the same distance.
When traveling to or from a smaller community, they are
likely to be cheaper than flying.

VIA Rail fares in Canada are somewhat more generous than
AMTRAK. Unlimited free stopovers are permitted and there
are unlimited mileage tickets available also.

In general, when traveling to a wilderness recreation
area away from a major city, it will be cheapest to use
intercity buses, with the train a close second. Airfare
to a small town is usually expensive compared to the
same distance flown between major cities. For instance,
to get to Cedar City, Utah, jumping-off point for Zion

GENERALIZED LEGEND FOR MAPS WITHIN BOOK

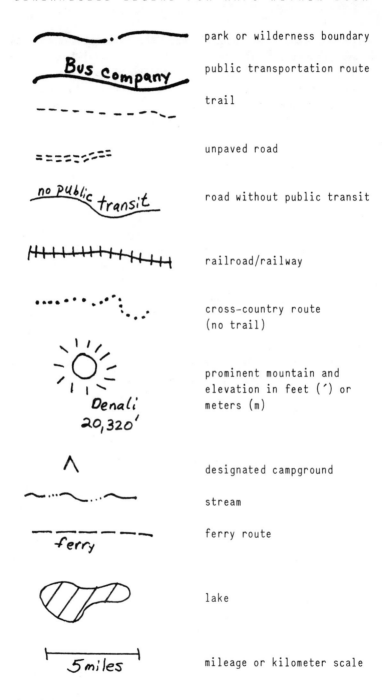

park or wilderness boundary

public transportation route

trail

unpaved road

road without public transit

railroad/railway

cross-country route
(no trail)

prominent mountain and
elevation in feet (′) or
meters (m)

designated campground

stream

ferry route

lake

mileage or kilometer scale

and Bryce Canyon National Parks, the greatest disparity between ground and air transportation costs will be found in flying to a smaller community such as Cedar City. It would be relatively economical to use any public transportation to get to Salt Lake City, but the intercity bus will be the cheapest way to get from Salt Lake to Cedar City.

OBTAINING THE MAPS YOU'LL NEED

The maps in this book are drawn to scale and will help orient you as you approach the trailhead. For your own safety, obtain a good map of your route before venturing out. Many of the trail guides in Appendix III have sufficient maps, but most people will prefer government topographic maps showing elevation changes and physical detail. Sources for U.S. and Canadian topographic maps are listed in Appendix VI. Index maps are available for each state or province, allowing you to determine which specific quadrangle is needed. You can also short circuit the process by going to a university library and photocopying their maps, if they can't be checked out.

Topographic maps from the United States Geological Survey (USGS) and the Canadian Surveys and Mappings Branch can also be purchased for a slight to exorbinant premium from backpacking equipment stores and from park and forest service visitor centers. In the United States, forest service visitor maps are full of information, but they normally lack topographic contours. Some of the newer maps for specific wilderness areas do show topographic contours however. Forest service maps can be obtained from the individual national forest or from the Regional Foresters whose addresses are also listed in Appendix VI. They currently cost one dollar each.

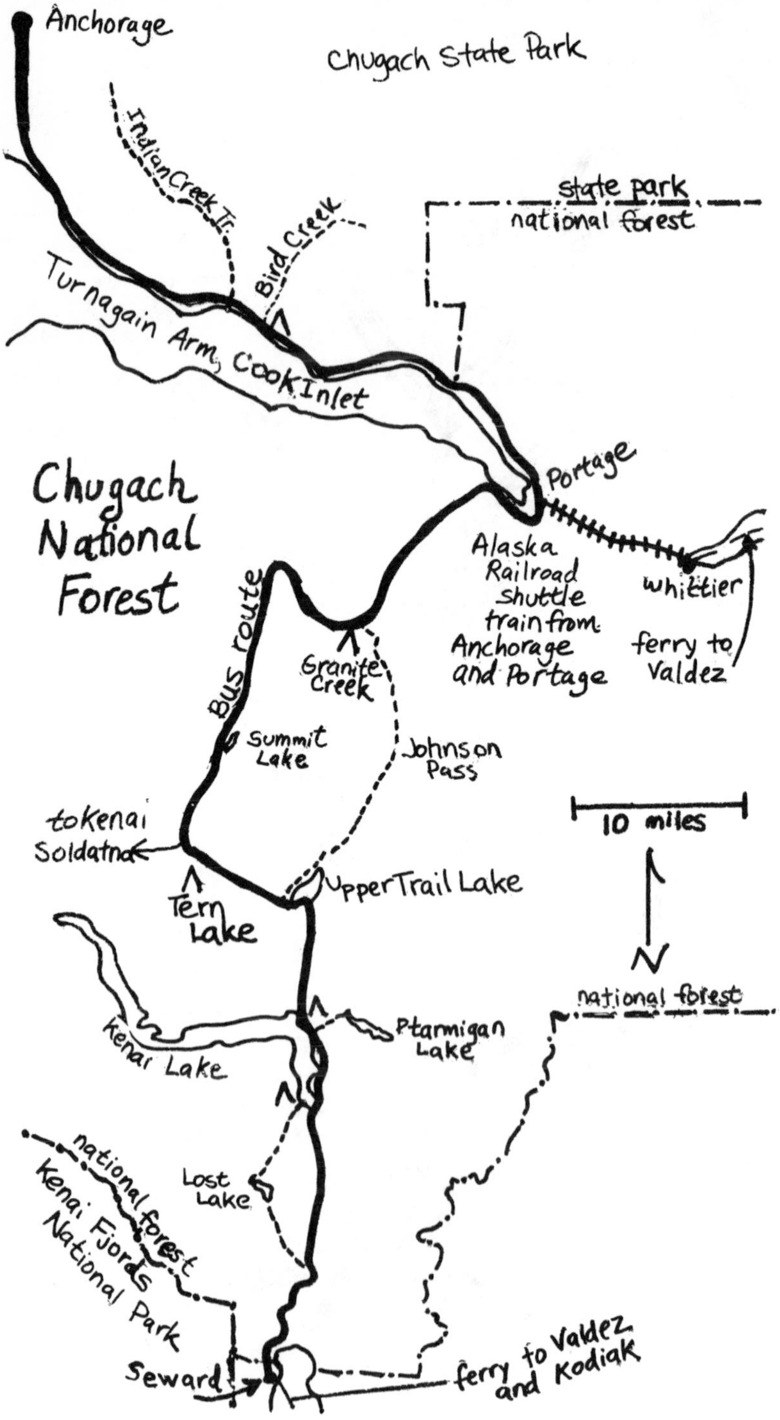

Anchorage
Chugach State Park
Indian Creek Tr.
Bird Creek
state park
national forest
Turnagain Arm, Cook Inlet
Portage
Chugach National Forest
Alaska Railroad shuttle train from Anchorage and Portage
whittier
ferry to Valdez
Bus route
Granite Creek
Summit Lake
Johnson Pass
10 miles
to Kenai Soldatna
Upper Trail Lake
Tern Lake
N
national forest
Ptarmigan Lake
Kenai Lake
Lost Lake
national forest
Kenai Fjords National Park
Seward
ferry to Valdez and Kodiak

CHUGACH NATIONAL FOREST

The Chugach National Forest is the second largest in
the United States; only the Tongass Forest in southeastern
Alaska covers more land. The Chugach Forest contains
mountain and ocean scenery as spectacular as any in Alaska
and the backcountry hiking opportunities are particularly
well developed.

The Seward Highway south of Anchorage, served by the
Seward Bus Line year round on a daily basis, provides
access to a number of trailheads. In Anchorage, the bus
can be picked up at the Anchorage Sheraton. Among the
popular hikes include the twenty-three mile Johnson Pass
Trail, which leaves the highway about a mile before Granite
Creek Campground and returns to the bus route at Upper
Trail Lake. The route climbs through Sitka spruce and
hemlock forest to two lakes at timberline on either side
of grass covered Johnson Pass. The Lost Lake Trail, several
miles north of Seward, is a seven mile hike through lush
coastal forest that leads to a meadow-bordered lake above
timberline.

From Seward, the Alaska Marine Highway System ferry MV
Tustumena provides regular service to Kodiak Island,
cruising past the tidewater glaciers of Kenai Fjords
National Park. Ferry service is also available from Seward
to Valdez, a trip that provides visual access to such
Chugach Forest attractions as Columbia Glacier and Prince
William Sound. More frequent ferry service to Valdez
is provided from Whittier, which can be reached by the
Alaska Railroad from Portage and Anchorage.

There is also currently summer bus service from Anchorage
to Kenai and Soldatna, which provides access to several
other trailheads. Because public transit service has
changed over the past few years, prospective hikers might
check with the Anchorage Convention and Visitors Bureau,
201 East 3rd Avenue (Zip: 99501) for updated bus schedules.

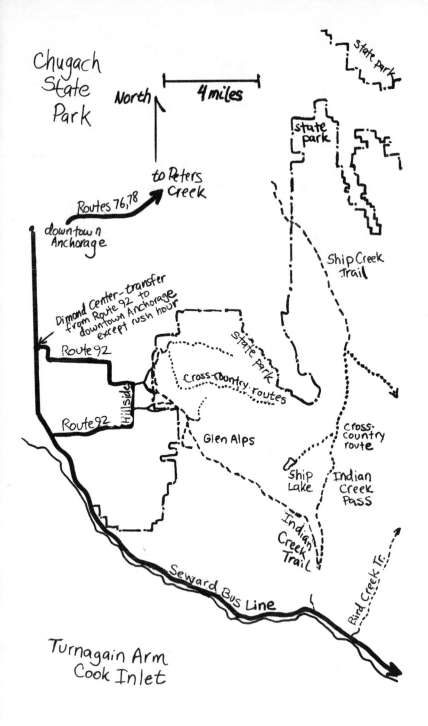

Chugach
State
Park

North

4 miles

to Peters
Creek

Routes 76,78

downtown
Anchorage

Dimond Center—transfer
from Route 92 to
downtown Anchorage
except rush hour

Route 92

Hillside

Route 92

state park

state park

state
park

Ship Creek
Trail

State Park

Cross-country routes

Glen Alps

cross-
country
route

Ship
Lake

Indian
Creek
Pass

Indian
Creek
Trail

Bird Creek Tr.

Seward Bus Line

Turnagain Arm
Cook Inlet

CHUGACH STATE PARK

Chugach State Park forms a spectacular mountain backdrop for the metropolitan Anchorage area. Within the one-half million acre park are trails leading to meadows, lakes and views of the glaciers beyond.

Anchorage Public Transit (The People Mover) Route 92 provides service six days weekly along Hillside Drive near the park boundary. Walking up either Upper Huffman Road or Upper O'Malley Road from Hillside Drive will lead to several trailheads in the Hillside Trail System of the Park. Another hike, up Peters Creek, is accessible from the turnaround point for Routes 76 and 78. As in the case of the Hillside Trail System, about a mile of road walking is necessary to reach the trailhead. Another possibility is to take one of the two buses that operate between Anchorage and Seward (see the Chugach National Forest entry) and get off at either Indian Creek (milepost 102, Seward Highway) or Bird Creek (milepost 100). Trails at both of these locations lead up streams into the Chugach Mountains. From Indian Creek it is possible to hike back to the Hillside Trail System served by The People Mover.

The downtown bus stop for The People Mover is at 7th Avenue and G Street. This is an uphill, but relatively short walk from the Alaska Railroad depot. Route 6 serves Anchorage International Airport.

Because of avalanche danger, the park headquarters should be consulted before embarking on winter trips.

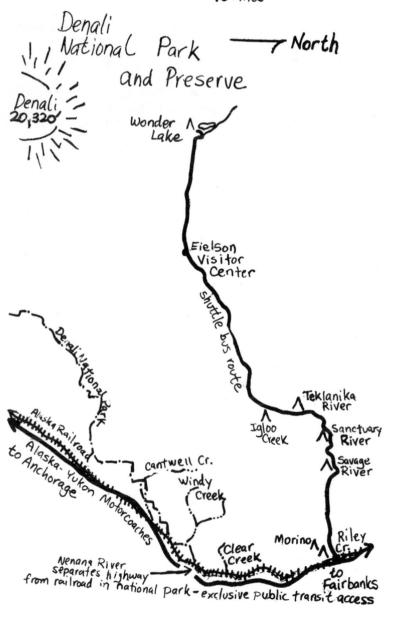

10 miles

Denali
National Park
and Preserve
North

Denali
20,320

Wonder
Lake

Eielson
Visitor
Center

Shuttle bus route

Denali National Park

Alaska Railroad

Alaska-Yukon Motorcoaches
to Anchorage

Cantwell Cr.

Windy
Creek

Teklanika
River

Igloo
Creek

Sanctuary
River

Savage
River

Morino

Riley
Cr.

Clear
Creek

Nenana River
separates highway
from railroad in national park - exclusive public transit access

to
Fairbanks

DENALI NATIONAL PARK AND PRESERVE

During Mt. McKinley's summer season, it is one of the few parks to actively encourage public transportation. Free (as of 1984) buses take park visitors along the park's only road, stopping to view wildlife and North America's highest mountain (weather permitting).

There are few designated trails, but hiking is easier along river bars and across alpine tundra. South of the Alaska Range, thick brush can limit progress and river crossings throughout the park are often a problem.

The Alaska Railroad provides transportation year round to the park from Anchorage and Fairbanks, with daily service in summer. Alaska-Yukon Motorcoaches also provide daily summer service from Fairbanks and Anchorage. Direct connections can be made onto the park bus system from the bus and train depot area. Also nearby is Riley Creek Visitor Center, fifteen minutes walk from the train station. Park personnel there can issue the required overnight permit. There are quotas established for overnight camping in the backcountry, but daytime use is largely unrestricted. Thus one efficient strategy for seeing the park is to use one or more of the seven established campgrounds as a base and use the shuttle bus to take a· different day hike each day. Morino Campground, near the train station, is limited to people without cars and is free.

A final possibility is to use the twice weekly local Alaska Railroad train that will stop anywhere on the tracks between Anchorage and Fairbanks. On the train southbound from Denali Park Station, hikes can be made west into the park, using streams such as Windy Creek, Clear Creek and Cantwell Creek as routes into the high country. Thick brush is the major problem, but once above treeline, hiking is easier. The Nenana River separates the train route from the highway, so this part of the park is restricted to train users.

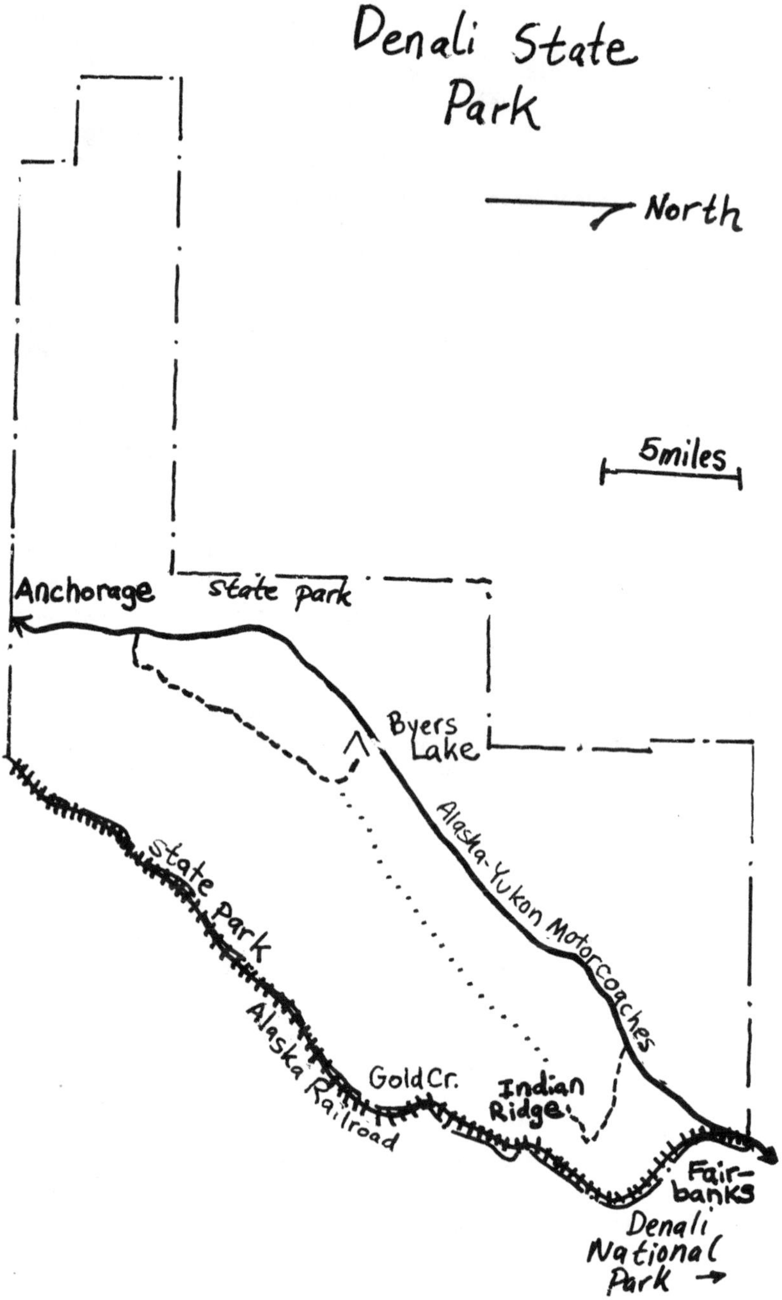

Denali State Park

North

5 miles

Anchorage

state park

Byers Lake

Alaska-Yukon Motorcoaches

State Park

Alaska Railroad

Gold Cr.

Indian Ridge

Fairbanks

Denali National Park →

DENALI STATE PARK

Denali State Park is largely undeveloped wilderness in the foothills of the Alaska Range and the Susitna and Chulitna River Valleys. The park is bisected by the Parks (Anchorage - Fairbanks) Highway, but public transportation users will be interested in the hiking and ski touring possibilities off the Alaska Railroad route on the eastern boundary of the park. Local trains, twice weekly in each direction in summer, and once weekly in each direction in winter, will stop anywhere on their route between Anchorage and Fairbanks, including the remote areas of Denali State and Denali National Parks away from roads.

The most common place to get off the train is just after the railroad crosses the Susitna River (northbound) at Gold Creek. A copy of the USGS map for the area (Talkeetna Mountains D-6) should be obtained beforehand because there are no facilities in this part of the park.

Two trails have been developed along the highway corridor. Little Coal Creek, starting at Mile 163.5, Parks Highway, reaches some beautiful alpine country on top of Indian Ridge with a panoramic view of Mt. McKinley across the Chulitna River Valley. Another fifteen mile long trail links Byers Lake Campground (Mile 147 on the highway) with Troublesome Creek (Mile 138). The Byers Lake end of the trail is linked to Little Coal Creek by a flagged route along the top of Indian Ridge. It is possible to reach this route atop Indian Ridge from the Alaska Railroad route although it is more difficult than from the highway. For bus transportation to the highway trailheads, contact Alaska-Yukon Motorcoaches beforehand; while these are not scheduled stops, their buses on the Anchorage-Denali Park-Fairbanks route are flexible about flag stops if given prior notice.

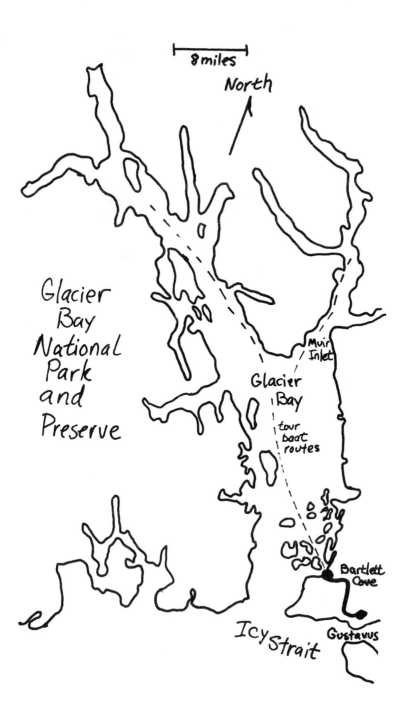

8 miles

North

Glacier
Bay
National
Park
and
Preserve

Glacier
Bay

tour
boat
routes

Muir
Inlet

Bartlett
Cove

Gustavus

Icy Strait

GLACIER BAY NATIONAL PARK AND PRESERVE

The fjords and tidewater glaciers of Glacier Bay limit hiking opportunities and kayaking has become a popular way of traversing the inlets of the park. Nevertheless many people fly to Gustavus from Juneau on Alaska Airlines (daily flights, summer only) with the intent of hiking in the park, one of the largest in the National Park System.

The park concessionaire provides bus transportation to the park headquarters from Gustavus. The only scheduled transportation from the park headquarters at Bartlett Cove to the tidewater glaciers is via daily tour boats. Backpackers and kayakers can be dropped off and picked up at pre-arranged times. After you have paid for this service, for the tour boat ride, the bus from Gustavus and the plane ride from Juneau, you will come to the conclusion that visiting Glacier Bay is fairly expensive. There are no public transportation services in the winter.

The jumping-off city of Juneau can be reached on several scheduled airlines and on the ferries of the Alaska Marine Highway System. City buses in Juneau do not serve either the Auke Bay ferry terminal or the airport; from the airport terminal walk a couple blocks to the Shop 'n Kart Supermarket to reach the busline. For Auke Bay ferry arrivals there are usually shuttles that meet the ferry, but reaching the more inexpensive public bus system requires a mile and a half walk.

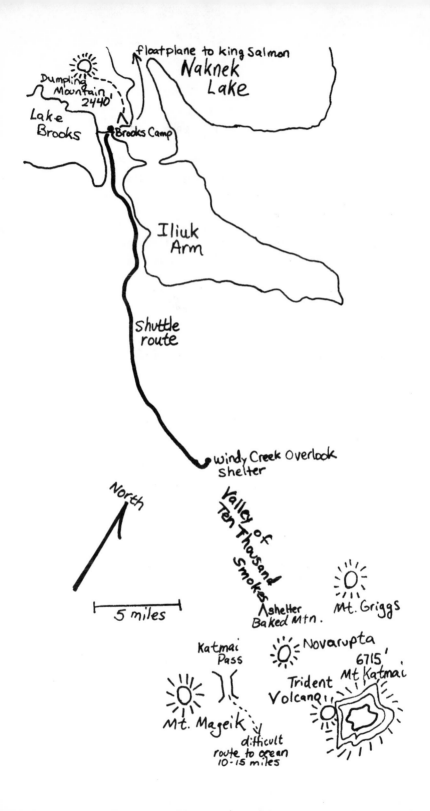

KATMAI NATIONAL PARK AND PRESERVE

One of the largest volcanic eruptions in recorded history
occurred in the area around Katmai in 1912 and the still
steaming volcanoes, along with trout and salmon fishing,
wildlife, fjords and isolation attract a small but growing
number of wilderness users.

The only scheduled transportation to this immense park
is via scheduled daily summer flights from Anchorage
to King Salmon (currently only MarkAir, check with a
travel agent for other carriers). A short connecting
flight via amphibious plane is made from King Salmon
to Naknek Lake where the park ranger station, a free
campground and the Brooks River Lodge is located. The
park concessionaire provides daily summer transportation
on an unimproved road to the Valley of Ten Thousand Smokes
from Naknek Lake. Trails are relatively non-existent,
but hiking is relatively easy on the ash-covered landscape.

Unlike Denali National Park and much of south-central
and southeastern Alaska, Katmai is out of the way, expensive
to get to, and the weather has a tendency not to cooperate.
It is nevertheless one of the most spectacular units
in the U.S. National Park System and there are few disap-
pointed visitors.

Silene acaulis

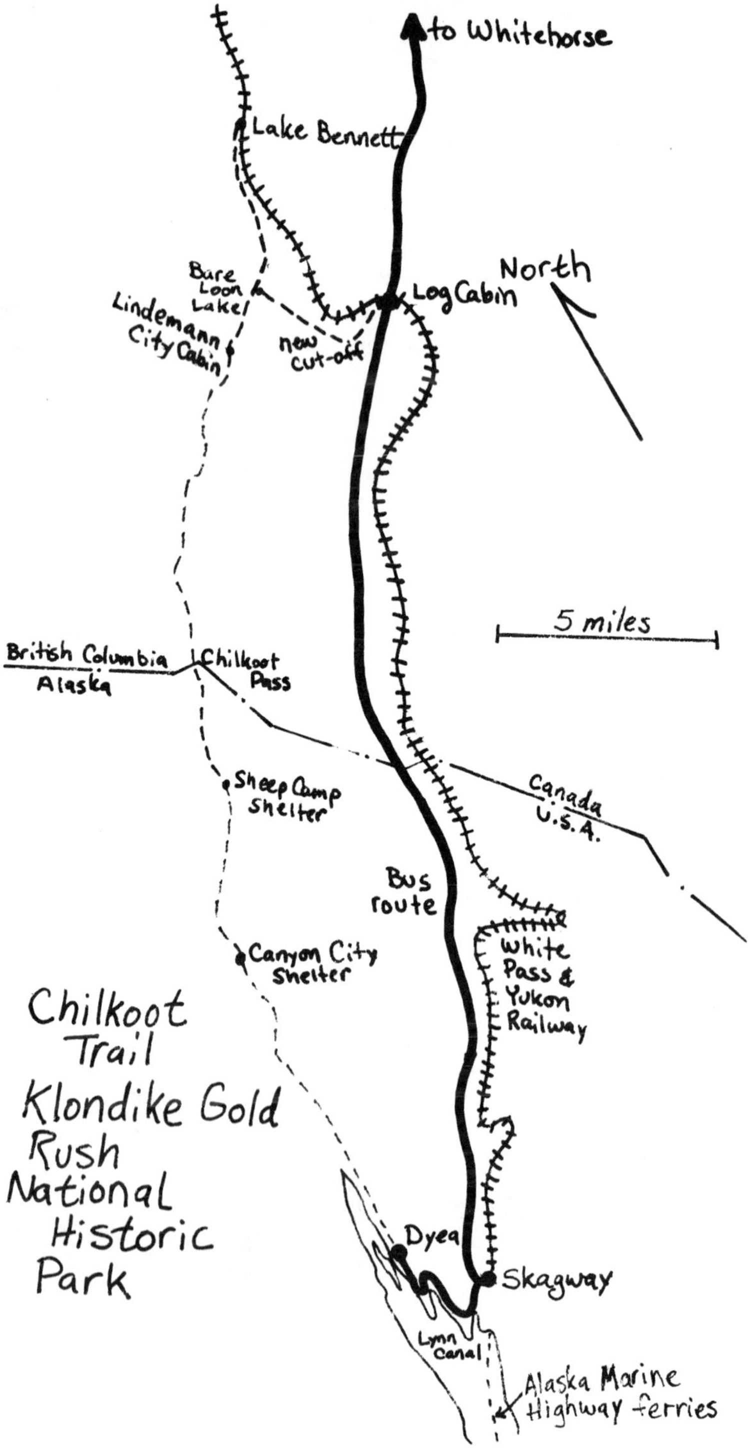

to Whitehorse

Lake Bennett

North

Bare Loon Lake

Lindemann City Cabin

Log Cabin

new cut-off

5 miles

British Columbia
Alaska

Chilkoot Pass

Sheep Camp Shelter

Canada
U.S.A.

Bus route

Canyon City Shelter

White Pass & Yukon Railway

Chilkoot Trail
Klondike Gold Rush National Historic Park

Dyea

Skagway

Lynn Canal

Alaska Marine Highway ferries

KLONDIKE GOLD RUSH NATIONAL HISTORIC PARK

The major route for hopeful gold miners heading to the Klondike Gold Rush was over Chilkoot Pass, now one of Alaska's best long distance backpacking trips. The thirty-two mile trail from Dyea to Lake Bennett is littered from the 1898 gold scramble and the beautiful mountain scenery is an added bonus.

The Alaska Marine Highway System serves Skagway and is the source of transportation for most hikers. Several agencies in Skagway are licensed to provide public transportation between Skagway and the official start of the trail in Dyea; check with the National Park Service office in town to determine the current available transportation. The other end of the hike at Lake Bennett was served by the White Pass and Yukon Railway, which had ceased operation during the summer of 1983 due to the depression of mineral prices, the railway's main source of revenue. Replacement bus service was being provided by Grayline of Alaska, although the situation could change if the railway re-starts service. Using the bus service, twice daily in each direction (summer only), requires leaving the traditional trail at Bare Loon Lake. A cut-off leads to the Klondike Highway at Log Cabin, British Columbia, where the bus can be picked up.

Crater Lake, east side of Chilkoot Pass

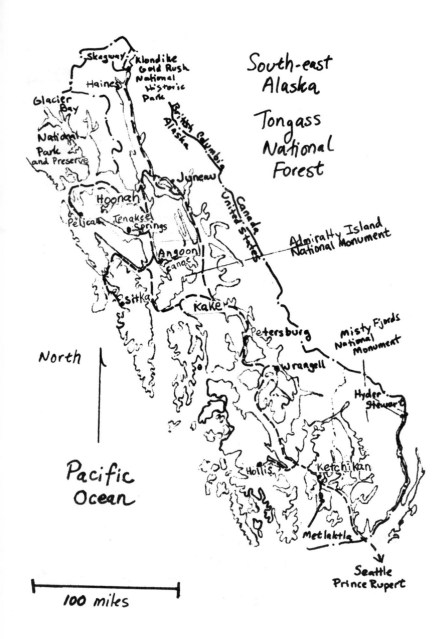

Skaguay
Klondike
Gold Rush
National
Historic
Park
Haines
Glacier
Bay
British
Columbia
Alaska
National
Park
and Preserve
Juneau
Hoonah
Pelican
Tenakee
Springs
Canada
United States
Admiralty Island
National Monument
Angoon
Canoe
Sitka
Kake
Petersburg
Misty Fjords
National
Monument
North
Wrangell
Hyder
Stewart
Pacific
Ocean
Hollis
Ketchikan
Metlaktla
Seattle
Prince Rupert
100 miles

South-east
Alaska

Tongass
National
Forest

TONGASS NATIONAL FOREST

The Tongass Forest is the largest national forest in the
United States, consisting of a wide variety of mountain
and marine environments. It is an area larger than many
states, so little justice can be given to all of the possible
outdoor activities. The Alaska Marine Highway System ferries
serve the area from Prince Rupert and Seattle. Ketchikan,
Wrangell, Petersburg, Sitka, Juneau, Haines and Skagway
are the main ports for the ferry system and these communities
also have scheduled airline service. Auxiliary ferries
serve a number of other communities, including Metlakatla,
Hollis, Kake, Angoon, Tenakee Springs, Hoonah and Pelican.
Skagway and Haines both have summer bus service. See the
Portland Canal description under British Columbia for
information on the year round bus service to Stewart.
This community and nearby Hyder are adjacent to Misty
Fjords National Monument, a separate unit within the forest.
Angoon is in another unit, Admiralty Island National Monu-
ment, which is noted for bald eagles, brown bears and
a 26 mile canoe route across the island.

Many southeast Alaska towns have formally developed trail
systems. Bring rubber boots to deal with muddy conditions;
for the most part, trails are short, rudimentary and steep.
Juneau is a good starting point because there is a city
bus system allowing visitors to get around and the Forest
Service has concentrated ski and hiking trail development
in this community, the largest population center in southeast
Alaska.

The U.S. Forest Service rents public recreation cabins
on lakes, ocean-front, and other scenic places throughout
the forest. Most require chartering of floatplanes or
boats to reach, but some, such as one outside of Skagway,
can be reached by trail. There are five cabins available
along the Angoon Island canoe route. The rental fees are
nominal, but the cabins have to be reserved well in advance.
They make a very welcome shelter in a climate subject
to as much rain as is southeast Alaska.

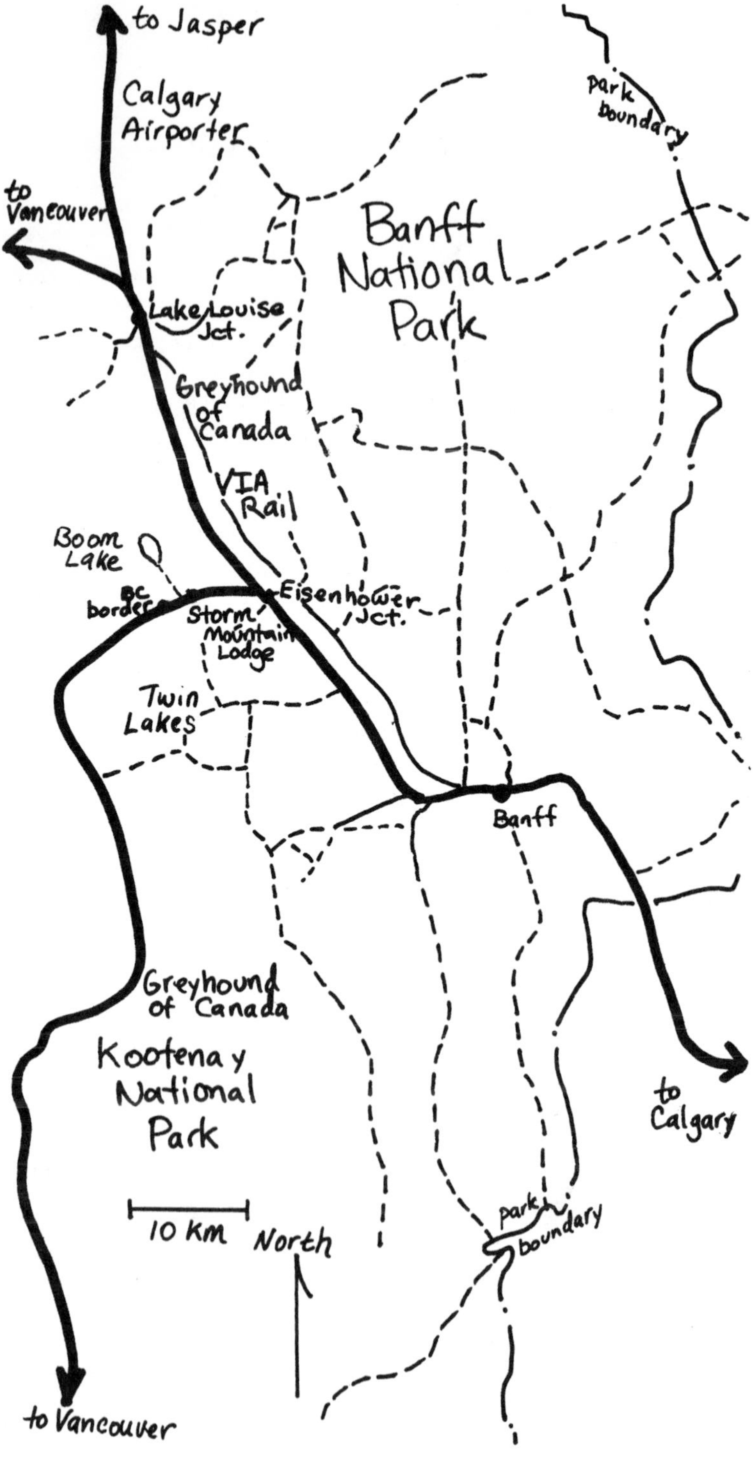

to Jasper

Calgary Airporter

to Vancouver

Banff National Park

Park boundary

Lake Louise Jct.

Greyhound of Canada

VIA Rail

Boom Lake

BC border

Eisenhower Jct.

Storm Mountain Lodge

Twin Lakes

Banff

Greyhound of Canada

Kootenay National Park

to Calgary

10 Km   North

park boundary

to Vancouver

BANFF NATIONAL PARK

A scenic highlight of the Rockies, Banff is one of Canada's most famous parks. Emerald colored lakes sit beneath glacier covered peaks and trails are relatively uncrowded.

The cross-Canada VIA Rail train that serves Calgary stops at Lake Louise Jct. and in Banff Townsite. Greyhound of Canada, on its Vancouver to Calgary route, stops at Lake Louise Junction, Eisenhower (Castle) Junction, and at Banff Townsite. The Calgary Airporter also provides summer service to the park from Calgary and Jasper. It is the only public transportation between Banff and Jasper National Park to the north; advance reservations are required. Once daily in each direction, Greyhound of Canada runs a bus on its Calgary to Vancouver route via Kootenay National Park. This bus has flag stops at Eisenhower (Castle Junction), Storm Mountain Lodge and the B.C. -Alberta border, as well as providing access to Kootenay National Park.

Storm Mountain Lodge is opposite the trailhead to Twin Lakes; another trail to these two lakes begins two hundred m east of Eisenhower Jct. From Lower Twin Lake, a trail extending over Gibbons Pass gives access to a wide range of long distance hiking opportunities. About three km from either Storm Mountain Lodge or the provincial boundary is the trailhead for the short five km hike to Boom Lake. Another ten km hike from Eisenhower Jct. leads past Silverton Falls to Rockbound Lake.

The actual trailheads are further away from Lake Louise Jct. and Banff Townsite. Nevertheless both areas have a wide variety of backpacking trails. One classic trip would be the hike from Lake Louise to Banff, using backcountry trails east of the Trans-Canada Highway.

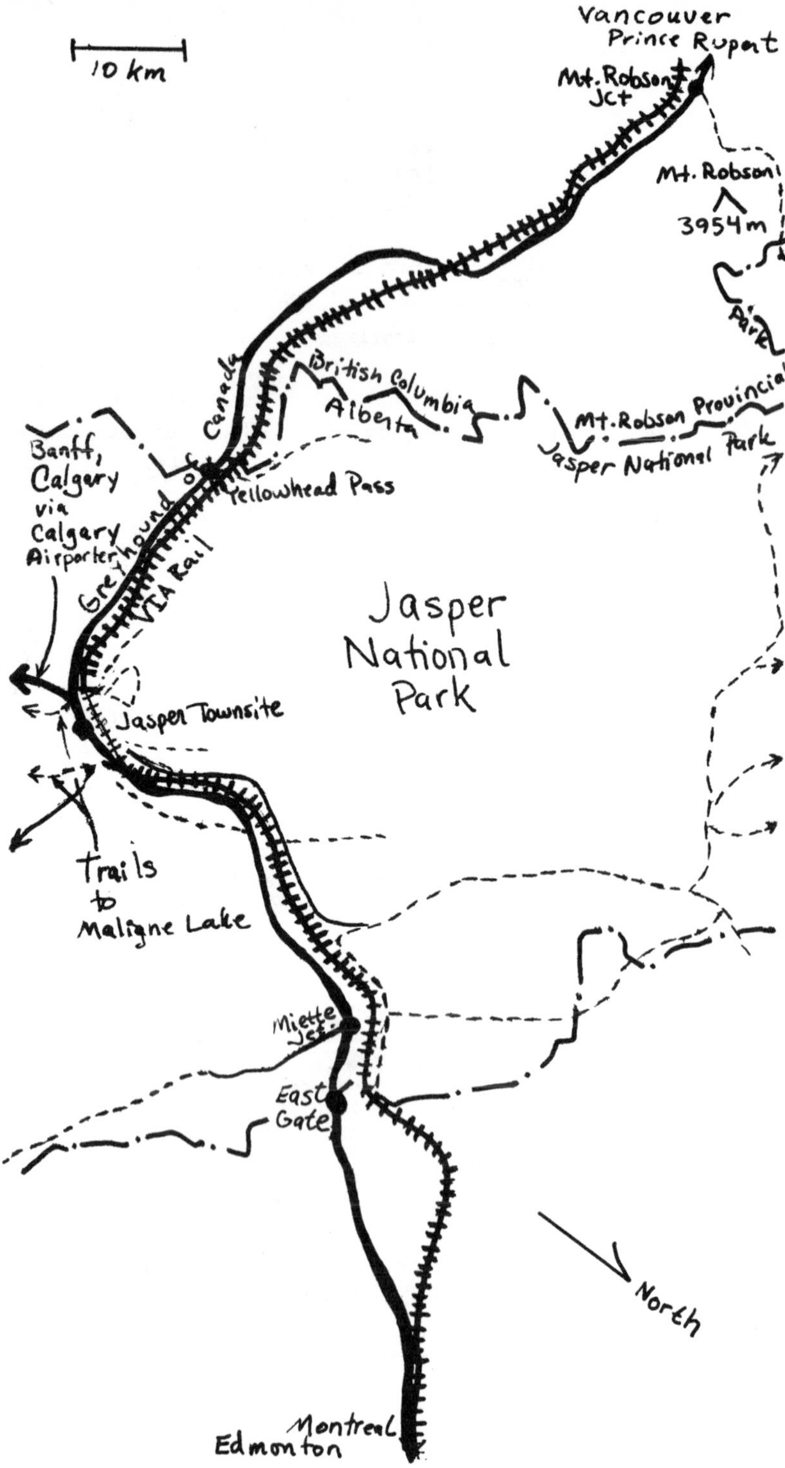

Vancouver
Prince Rupert

Mt. Robson
Jct

10 km

Mt. Robson
3954 m

Canada

British Columbia

Alberta

Mt. Robson Provincial

Banff,
Calgary
via
Calgary
Airporter

Greyhound

VIA Rail

Yellowhead Pass

Jasper National Park

Jasper
National
Park

Jasper Townsite

Trails
to
Maligne Lake

Miette
Jct.

East
Gate

North

Montreal
Edmonton

JASPER NATIONAL PARK

Jasper is the largest of all parks on the spine of the Rockies, with an almost unlimited array of outdoor activities available year round.

On its Edmonton-Jasper-Vancouver route, Greyhound of Canada makes stops at the East Park Gate, Miette Junction, Jasper Townsite, Yellowhead Pass and Mt. Robson. VIA Rail makes a stop at Jasper on its transcontinental route (via Edmonton), and the Calgary Airporter provides summer service to Jasper from Calgary. Advance reservations are required for the airporter service; it is the only direct connection between Jasper and Banff National Park to the south for public transportation users.

Several short backpacking and hiking trails are available from the town of Jasper and a trail with unbridged river crossings leads north from Yellowhead Pass. Three kilometers from the Mt. Robson Greyhound stop is the start of the classic eighteen kilometer hike to Berg Lake, which sits two and a half vertical kilometers beneath Mt. Robson, the Canadian Rockies' highest peak. Berg Lake is actually in British Columbia's Mt. Robson Provincial Park and no permit is necessary for the hike. A Jasper National Park backcountry permit is required to hike beyond Berg Lake or in any other portion of the national park overnight. This permit for backcountry hiking can be obtained at the park office in Jasper. Quotas limiting the number of people using specific trails are also in effect.

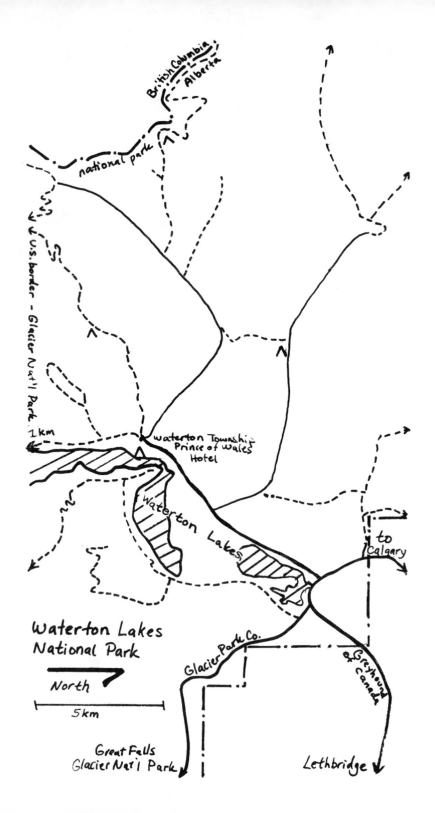

British Columbia
Alberta

national park

U.S. border - Glacier Nat'l Park

1 km

Waterton Township
Prince of Wales
Hotel

Waterton Lakes

to
Calgary

Waterton Lakes
National Park

North

5km

Glacier Park Co.

Greyhound Canada

Great Falls
Glacier Nat'l Park

Lethbridge

WATERTON LAKES NATIONAL PARK

Waterton Lakes is the northern half of the Glacier-Waterton Lakes International Peace Park. While it does not contain as extensive a trail system as Glacier Park, it does have a large backcountry area that is relatively lightly used.

Greyhound of Canada provides summer service to the park from Calgary and Lethbridge, Alberta. The best hiking in the park centers around the Waterton Township area, which is also accessible by using the bus service provided by Glacier Park, Inc. from Glacier Park Lodge in East Glacier, Montana. This summer service is to the Prince of Wales Hotel in Waterton Township. East Glacier is served daily by AMTRAK on its Chicago-Seattle Empire Builder route.

Waterton Lakes

1 mile

→ North

National Park Service
Shuttle available
summer only
West Rim
Dr.

Hermit's Rest

Bright Angel Lodge (bus terminal)

Bright Angel Trail to Colorado River

Nava-Hopi Tours

Served by shuttle

bus NPS-free

To Flagstaff

Williams

Canyon Rim

Visitor Center

store, bank, post office

Mather Campground

South Rim Grand Canyon National Park

East Rim Drive

South Kaibab Trail to canyon floor (steeper and shorter than Bright Angel Trail)

GRAND CANYON NATIONAL PARK

The bus trip out of Flagstaff or Williams winds across the ponderosa pine country of northern Arizona, not revealing the great chasm until the end of the bus ride. Like an incredible suprise, the canyon unveils itself to the first-time visitor. The Bright Angel Trail starts less than a hundred yards from the final bus stop of the Nava-Hopi Tours bus that provides daily service, year round, from both Flagstaff and Williams. Flagstaff has the AMTRAK connection and it is also served by both Greyhound and Trailways. Williams is also served by both Greyhound and Trailways.

There are two developed and maintained trails to the canyon floor from the South Rim. The Bright Angel Trail is closer to the bus terminal although the Kaibab Trail is shorter, albeit steeper, in distance from canyon rim to canyon floor. Both trails meet near a suspension bridge over the Colorado River and continue to the North Rim as one trail. There are also a number of other unmaintained trails that are more challenging to hike; consult a guidebook or the backcountry reservations office for more information. Permits for hiking are limited and it is advisable to write or phone ahead for more information. Hiking in the summer is likely to be very hot and water is limited at all times of the year.

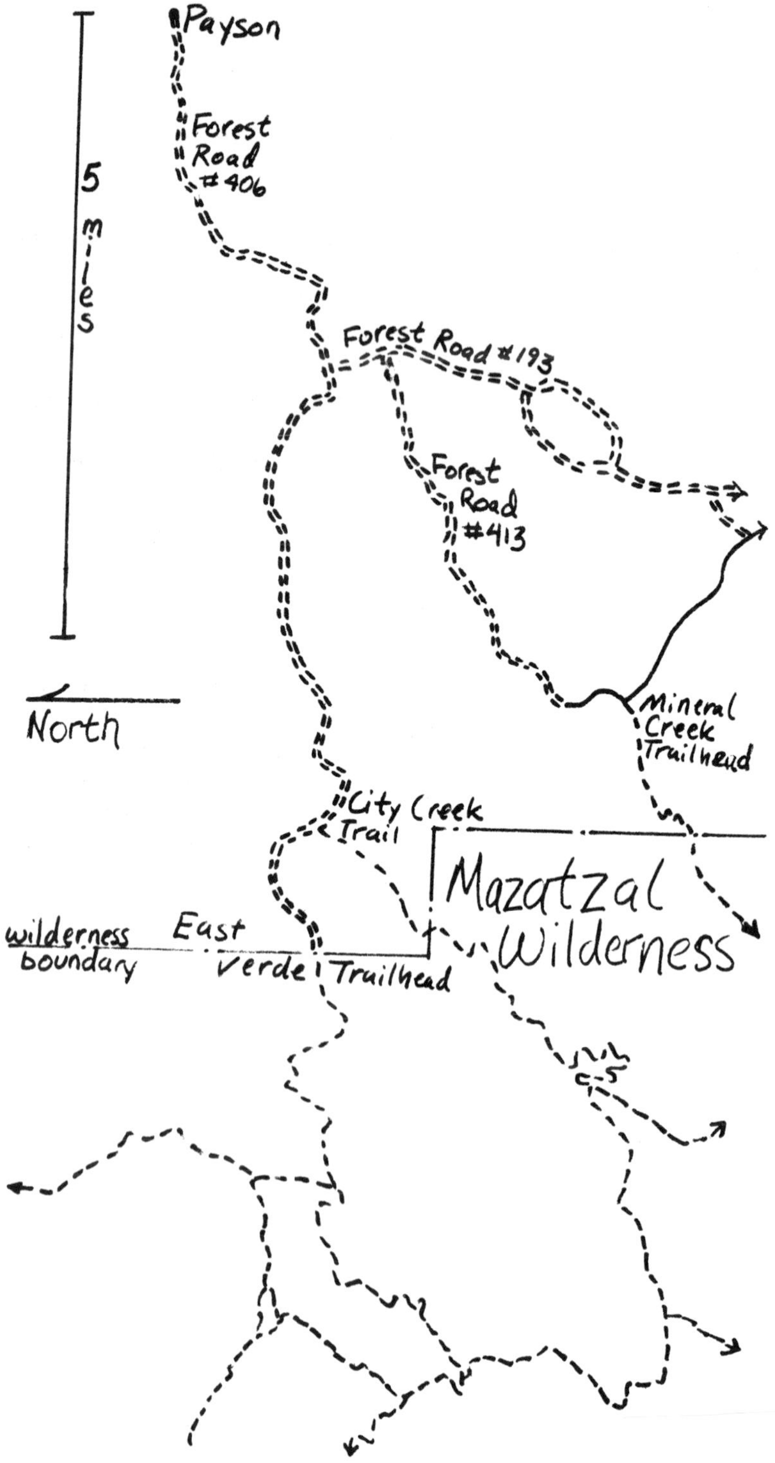

Payson

Forest
Road
#406

Forest Road #193

Forest
Road
#413

5
m
i
l
e
s

North

Mineral
Creek
Trailhead

City Creek
Trail

Mazatzal
Wilderness

wilderness
boundary

East
Verde

Trailhead

MAZATZAL WILDERNESS

An area of precipitious peaks and dry ridges, the Mazatzal Wilderness has a quiet appeal, prompted by isolating topography and desert climate. Plan to bring water with you.

It is possible to reach the wilderness by hiking out of Payson, served once daily, except Sundays and holidays, from Phoenix and Holbrook by White Mountain Lines. Holbrook is served by Greyhound and Trailways; Phoenix has these bus lines, as well as AMTRAK and major airline service.

Extending out of Payson are a network of unimproved roads which travel about ten miles to the wilderness boundary. At the end of Forest Service Road #406 are the East Verde Trailhead and the City Creek Trailhead. The East Verde Trail leads west to the East Verde River and provides access to several other trails, including one that loops back to the City Creek Trail. Also in this area, at the end of Forest Service Road #413, is the Mineral Creek Trail.

Currently no permits are required for entry into the wilderness, a lightly used area.

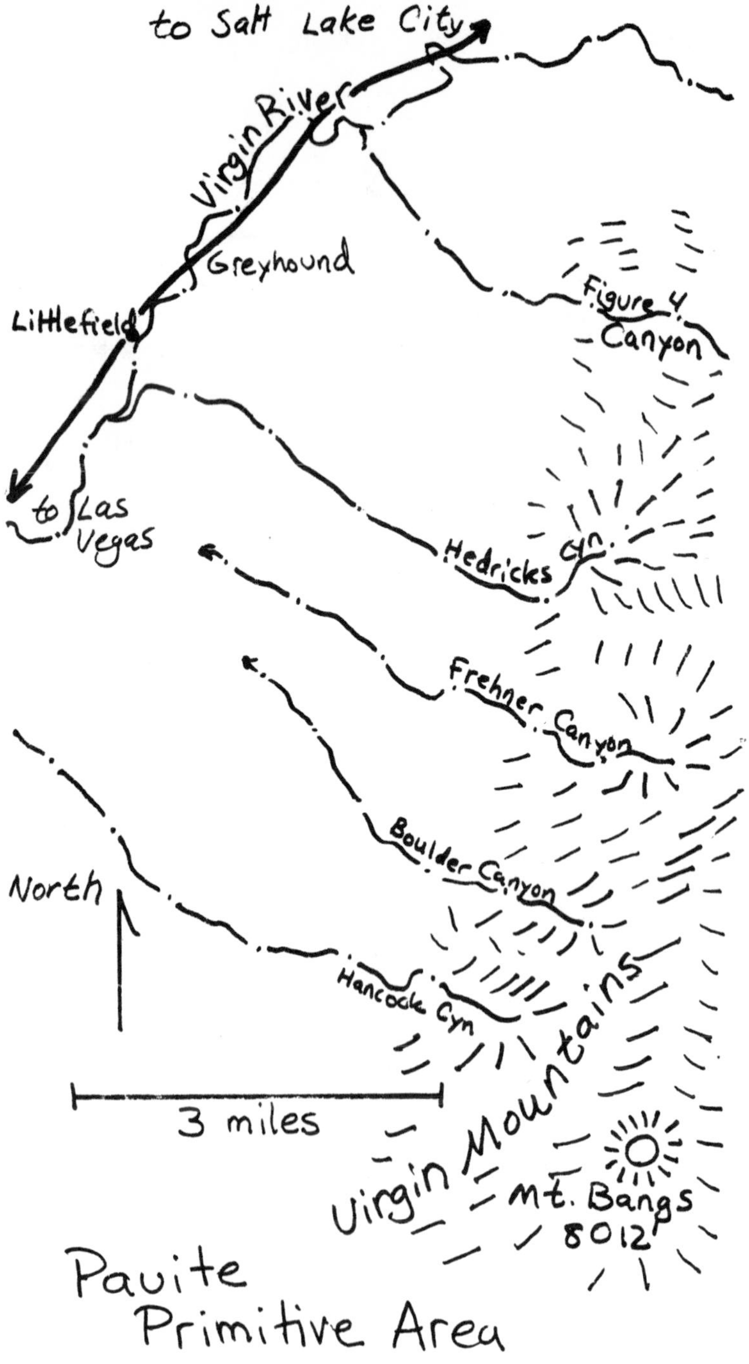

to Salt Lake City

Virgin River

Greyhound

Littlefield

to Las Vegas

Figure 4 Canyon

Hedricks Cyn.

Frehner Canyon

Boulder Canyon

North

Hancock Cyn

3 miles

Virgin Mountains

Mt. Bangs 8012

Pauite Primitive Area

PAUITE PRIMITIVE AREA

Across the Virgin River from the town of Littlefield are
the Virgin Mountains, which make up the bulk of this roadless
area, managed by the Bureau of Land Management. The highest
peak in the range, Mt. Bangs, is over 8000 feet in elevation
and the elevation in Littlefield is around 2000 feet.
There are no trails in the Littlefield area to encourage
visitors and the lack of water and high summer temperatures
should work to keep this area quiet. Nevertheless, this
area does have a wild, untrodden quality and this will
serve as inducement enough for those who venture into
the Virgin Mountains. Greyhound has one highway stop per
day in each direction on its Salt Lake City-Las Vegas
route.

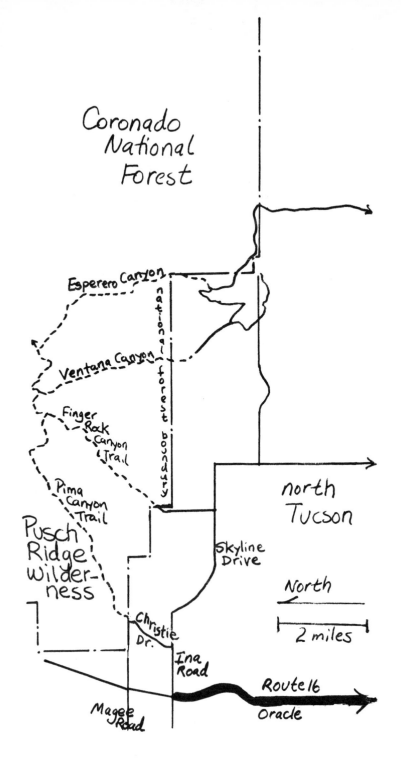

PUSCH RIDGE WILDERNESS

A new wilderness in the Santa Catalina Mountains near Tucson, Pusch Ridge consists of high peaks, snow covered in winter, and rising above the Sonoran desert. It can be reached using Tucson's Sun-Trans bus system.

The sprawling nature of the Tucson metropolitan area makes public transit use somewhat of a challenge, but the Route 16 bus can be taken to the corner of Ina Road and Oracle six days a week and this will put the hiker within three miles of the Pima Canyon Trailhead. To reach the trail, walk east on Ina Road one mile and then northeast on Christie Drive one and a half miles to Magee Road. The trail begins at the end of Magee Road, a short distance to the east. Tucson International Airport is served by Sun-Trans Route 8 and AMTRAK serves Tucson on its Los Angeles-New Orleans route.

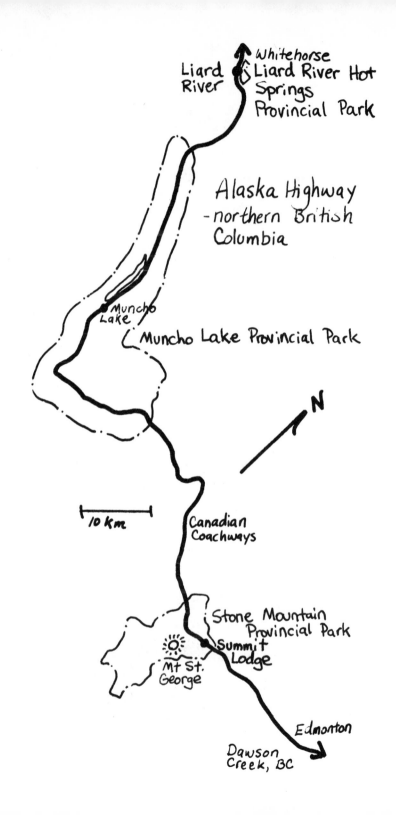

ALASKA HIGHWAY - BRITISH COLUMBIA

The most scenic portion of the Alaska Highway within British
Columbia is that portion that traverses the northernmost
section of the Rocky Mountains about 400 km west of the
highway initiation in Dawson Creek, B.C. This is a wild
and unpopulated region, short on facilities, so bring
the food and supplies needed. Canadian Coachways, a Greyhound
associated company, has bus service several days per week
year round from Dawson City to Whitehorse, with connecting
service to Edmonton and Vancouver.

The bus route on the Alaska Highway includes stops at
Summit Lodge, Muncho Lake and Liard River. Summit Lodge
is 1.5 km east of the highest pass on the highway, 1295
meters. This immediate area is within Stone Mountain Provincial Park, a 25,600 hectare preserve. The highway is close
to timberline here and there are few obstacles to the
tops of the nearby 2000 meters peaks. A large glaciated
area to the south, including the peaks Roosevelt, Churchill
and Stalin (the highest at 2896 meters) is visible from
higher vantage points.

Further west, Muncho Lake is within Muncho Lake Provincial
Park, a 87,384 hectare park. As in Stone Mountain Park,
there is little in the way of formalized trails. One route
about 13 km in length follows Nonda Creek, but it is unfortunately nearly thirty km from the bus stop at Muncho Lake.
Closer to the bus stop are other less defined trails which
parallel the Trout River. Also near the Muncho Lake bus
stop are overnight accomodations, provincial campgrounds
and fishing opportunities.

The bus stop at Liard River Lodge is located within walking
distance of Liard River Hot Springs, a smaller provincial
park with camping and sulfur springs open year round.

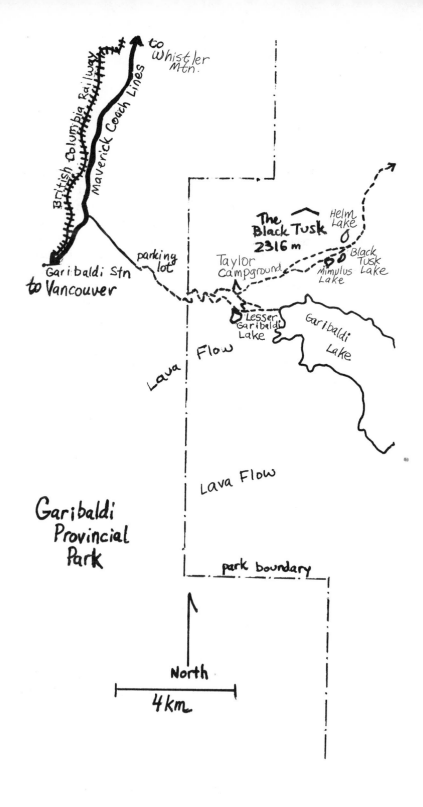

GARIBALDI PROVINCIAL PARK

Garibaldi Park encompasses the final northward extension
of Cascade volcanic activity. Close to metropolitan Vancouver, it is a popular destination and has much to offer
in the way of alpine hiking.

Maverick Coachlines and the British Columbia Railway both
stop at Garibaldi Station daily. One of the park's major
trailheads can be reached by walking north three kilometers
on Highway 99 to the Black Tusk Recreation Area turnoff,
turning right and proceeding two and a half kilometers
to the parking lot and trailhead. Taylor Creek Cabin is
reached after seven kilometers of hiking and a variety
of destinations are available from there.

Crosscountry skiing and snowshoeing are possible in winter
and Maverick Coachlines has additional service during
the ski season. Unfortunately the snow level may be above
the bus and train stations.

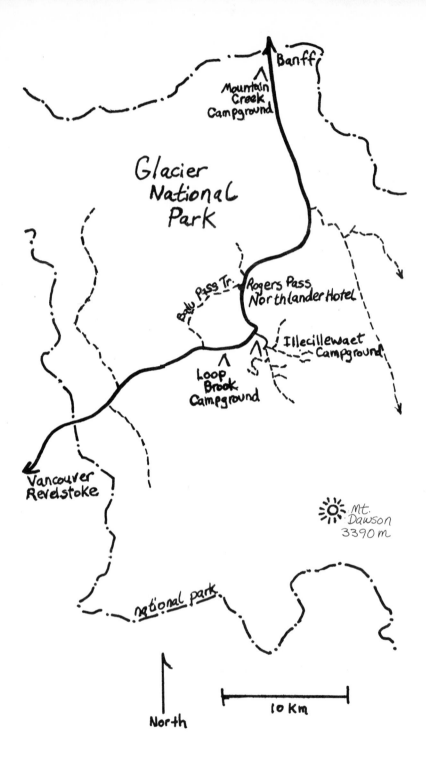

Glacier National Park

Banff

Mountain Creek Campground

Bally Pass Tr.

Rogers Pass
Northlander Hotel

Illecillewaet Campground

Loop Brook Campground

Vancouver Revelstoke

Mt. Dawson
3390 m

national park

North

10 Km

GLACIER NATIONAL PARK

Canada's Glacier National Park, set in the weathered Selkirk
Mountains midway between the Coast Range and the Rockies,
is besieged by heavy snows that feed the park's glaciers.
Grizzly bears are probably as common here as anyplace
in North America. Several hiking possibilities are available
from the Greyhound of Canada stop at Rogers Pass.

The Balu Pass trail starts at the north end of the Northlander Hotel parking lot at Rogers Pass. This can either
be a nice one-way hike to the pass summit (five kilometers)
or the hike can be continued into Cougar Valley ending
up on the Trans-Canada Highway nine kilometers west of
Rogers Pass. A good base for day hiking is the Illecillewaet
Campground which is about four kilometers west of Rogers
Pass on the Trans-Canada Highway.

Crosscountry skiing is popular in winter, but there is
often a high avalanche danger.

Mt. Sir Donald from Abbott Ridge Trail

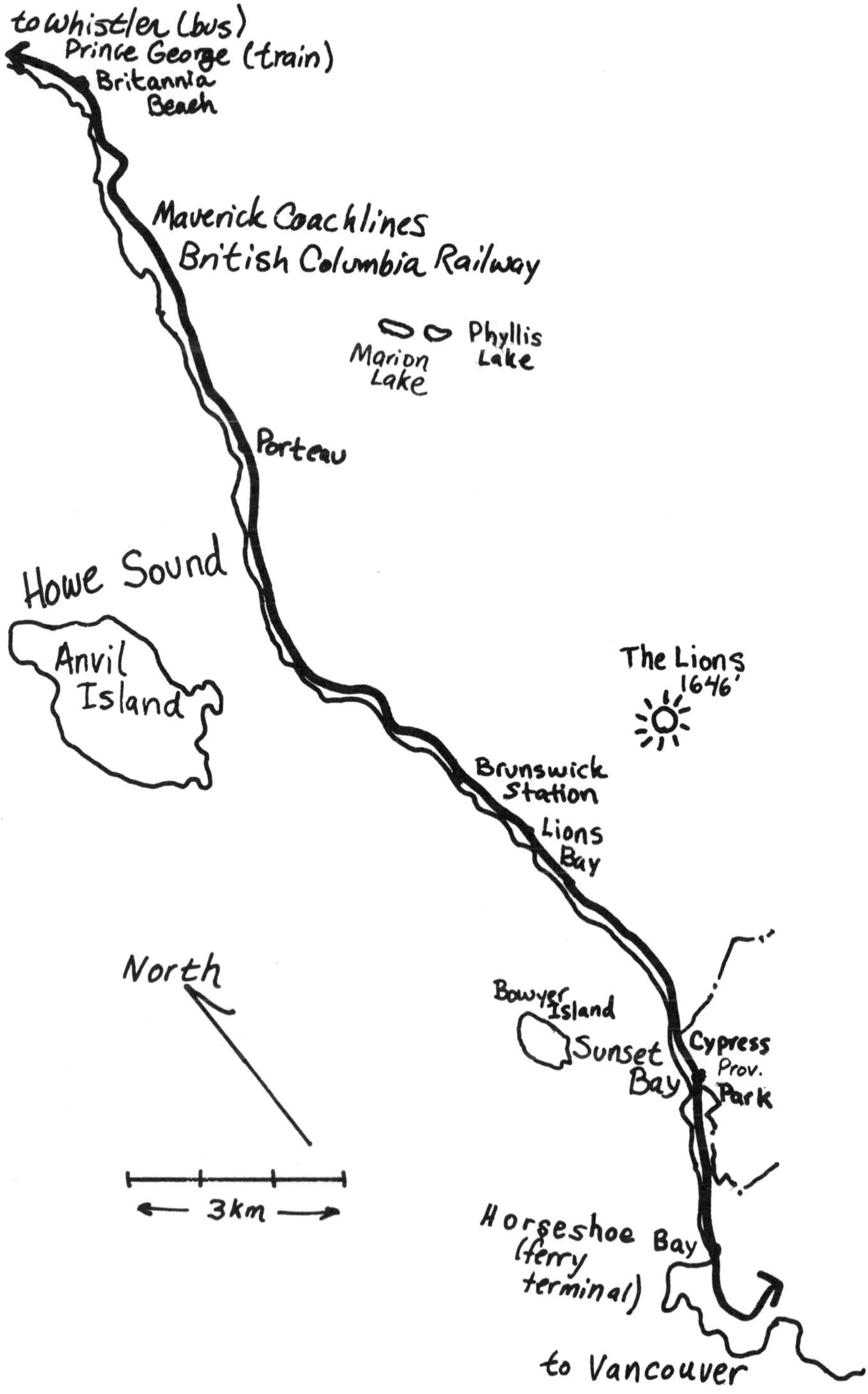

to Whistler (bus)
Prince George (train)
Britannia
Beach

Maverick Coachlines
British Columbia Railway

Marion   Phyllis
Lake   Lake

Porteau

Howe Sound

Anvil
Island

The Lions
1646'

Brunswick
Station

Lions
Bay

North

Bowyer
Island
Sunset
Bay

Cypress
Prov.
Park

3km

Horseshoe Bay
(ferry
terminal)

to Vancouver

HOWE SOUND

At the backdoor of Vancouver, coastal mountains provide
a number of possible hikes. Most trails climb steeply
into the forested mountains overlooking scenic Howe Sound.
Many trailheads are poorly marked, but the book, 103
Hikes in Southwestern British Columbia (The Mountaineers,
Seattle), gives good explicit directions.

Maverick Coach Lines and the British Columbia Railway
are the two sources of public transportation. Both serve
Lions Bay from Vancouver; an unpaved road turning off
Highway 99 at Lions Bay switchbacks up to the trailhead
for the hike to Mt. Unnecessary, eight km away at 1554
m high. West and East Lion and other alpine high points
are available beyond.

The trail to Black Mountain, part of the forty-two kilometer
Vancouver Skyline Trail, can be reached from the railway
or bus stop at Horseshoe Bay. The trail starts just past
the ferry turnoff on Highway 99.

Trails to Cypress Bowl and Yew Lake are accessible from
Sunset Bay, a railway stop; the trail to Deeks Lake is
four kilometers north on Highway 99 from the Brunswick
rail stop; the trail to Marion and Phyllis Lakes is four
kilometers north by road from the Porteau train station;
Petgill Lake trail is five kilometers north of the Britannia
Beach rail stop, off Highway 99.

Maverick Coach Lines also has another route, from Vancouver
to Powell River, via the Horseshoe Bay ferry. A number
of bus stops, including Langdale, Gibsons, Roberts Creek,
Sechelt, Halfmoon Bay, Secret Cove and Earl Cove are
close to hiking spots, some of which can be overnight
trips. Hiking Trails of the Sunshine Coast (Harbour Publishing, Madeira Park, BC/Signpost Books, Edmonds, WA) is
a good source of trip suggestions.

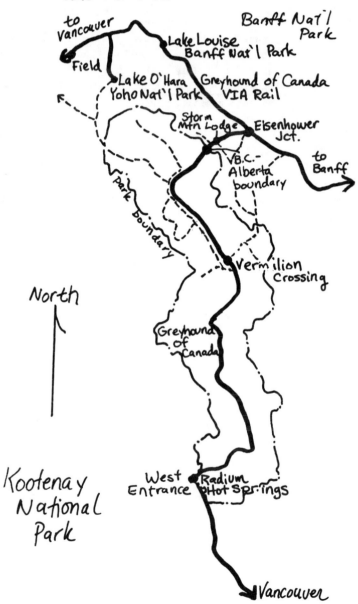

10 Km

Yoho Nat'l Park

to Vancouver

Field

Lake Louise
Banff Nat'l Park

Banff Nat'l Park

Lake O'Hara
Yoho Nat'l Park

Greyhound of Canada
VIA Rail

Storm
Mtn Lodge

Eisenhower
Jct.

to Banff

B.C.-
Alberta
boundary

Park Boundary

Vermilion
Crossing

North

Greyhound
of
Canada

Kootenay
National
Park

West
Entrance

Radium
Hot Springs

Vancouver

KOOTENAY NATIONAL PARK

Lesser known sister park to Banff, Jasper and Yoho, Kootenay shares their spectacular scenery. Partly because it is less crowded, it is a good objective for backpacking, ski touring and snowshoeing.

Greyhound of Canada's Calgary-Banff-Radium-Vancouver route goes through the park once daily in each direction and makes three stops: Vermilion Crossing, Radium Hot Springs and the West Entrance to the park. The Vermilion Crossing area has opportunities for long distance hiking and the other two stops are close to hot springs, the park head-quarters and Redstreak Campground.

Kaufmann Lake

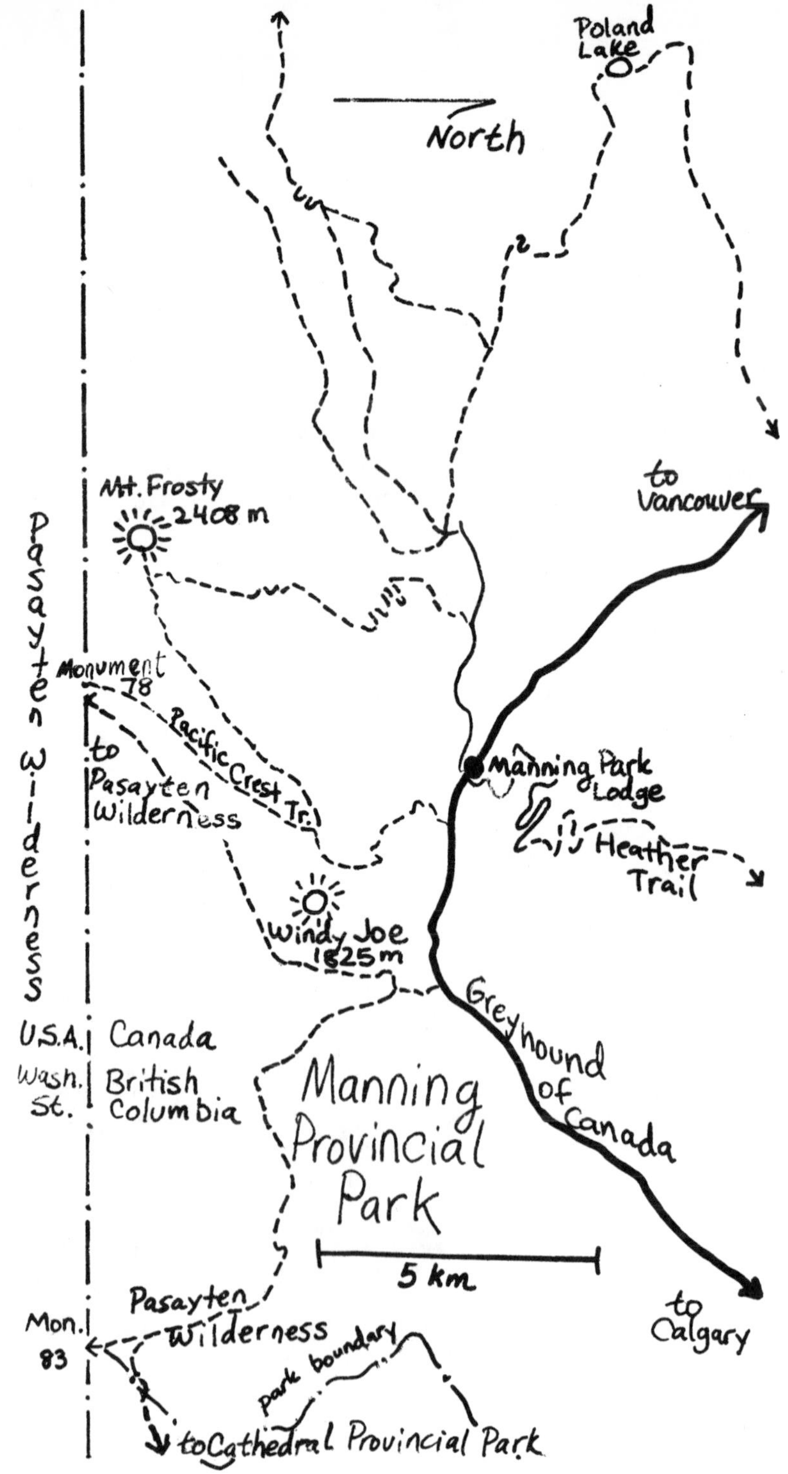

Poland Lake
North
to Vancouver
Mt. Frosty 2408 m
Pasayten Wilderness
Monument 78
to Pasayten Wilderness
Pacific Crest Tr.
Manning Park Lodge
Heather Trail
Windy Joe 1825 m
Greyhound of Canada
U.S.A.
Canada
Wash. St.
British Columbia
Manning Provincial Park
5 km
to Calgary
Pasayten Wilderness
Mon. 83
park boundary
to Cathedral Provincial Park

MANNING PROVINCIAL PARK

Directly north of North Cascades National Park and the Pasayten Wilderness in Washington, Manning Park preserves the Canadian extension of the North Cascades. Ski touring and snowshoeing trails are marked in winter and the park is popular for the rugged, jumbled mountains that characterize the North Cascades.

Greyhound of Canada, on its Vancouver to Calgary route, stops four times daily in each direction at Manning Park Lodge. Access to the northern terminus of the U.S. Pacific Crest Trail and to other hiking within the park is available by walking east one km along the highway and turning right onto the trail towards Windy Joe. It is seven km to Windy Joe, elevation 1825 meters; other trails lead to the top of Mt. Frosty (2408 meters) and to Monument 78 at the U.S. border. Inside the detachable metal monument marking the international boundary are the notes and journal entries of numerous individuals who have walked the trail from Mexico.

Additional hiking trails, to a campsite at Poland Lake (eight km one way), and along the twenty-one km Heather Trail are also close to Manning Park Lodge.

In addition to the Pacific Crest Trail, another trail that enters Washington's Pasayten Wilderness is the one which crosses the border at Monument 83. A loop trip of 54 km is possible, with 25 km within the uncrowded Pasayten, Washington's largest designated wilderness, before a return to Manning Park via the Pacific Crest Trail. The Monument 83 trail also provides access to a 84 km one way trail into Cathedral Provincial Park to the east.

Vancouver

Revelstoke

5 km

North

Mt. Revelstoke
1943 m

National park

shelter

Greyhound of Canada

Upper
Lower Jade Lakes

Clachnacudian
Snowfield

West Gate

Mt. Klotz
2598 m

Mt. Revelstoke
National Park

national park

Banff
Glacier Parks

MT. REVELSTOKE NATIONAL PARK

A relatively small park set in the weathered Selkirk Mountains, Mt. Revelstoke is nevertheless very accessible and provides several worthwhile hiking possibilities. It contains a wide range of biological communities because of altitude changes that extend to the glaciated summits.

Greyhound of Canada and VIA Rail both stop in the town of Revelstoke. Near the corner of Victoria Road and Garden Avenue, on the north side of the train tracks, a trail starts which reaches the summit of Mt. Revelstoke (1943 meters), a destination also reached by road. Additional hiking away from the road is accessible from the summit of Mt. Revelstoke and from the West Gate Entrance, which is a Greyhound of Canada flag stop passed daily by five buses in each direction on the Vancouver to Calgary route.

Port Alberni
by ferry
Kildonan
Vancouver Island
year-round
route
West
Coast Trail
by request
Saturdays
Gibralter
Island
Bamfield
Broken
Group
Islands
Pacific Rim
National Park
MV Lady Rose
Vancouver
Island
Summer
route
Pacific
Ocean
Port Alberni
by road
Orient
Stage
Lines
Ucluelet
Tofino
Long Beach
North
10Km

PACIFIC RIM NATIONAL PARK

A new park on the stormy west coast of Vancouver Island, Pacific Rim has three components: the sandy stretch of Long Beach, the Broken Group Islands, and the West Coast Trail. The West Coast Trail is a seventy-five kilometer route that was originally constructed to aid shipwrecked mariners in reaching civilization. Much of the trail is overgrown and remains a challenge to hike, taking a week or more.

The north end of the trail at Bamfield can be reached using the MV Lady Rose, operated by Alberni Marine Transportation. The ship sails down Alberni Inlet from Port Alberni three times weekly, with additional Sunday service in July and August. Port Alberni can be reached from Victoria and Nanaimo (Vancouver ferry connections) via several daily Vancouver Island Coach Line buses. In addition to serving the West Coast Trail at Bamfield, Ucluelet, near the Long Beach section of the park, is served three times weekly from June 1 to September 30. This route involves sailing through the Broken Group Islands and a stop is made at Gibralter Island where canoes and kayaks can be unloaded. There is primitive camping available as well as limited amounts of fresh water. There is no scheduled stop at Gibralter Island except in summer, but the year round sailing to Bamfield will stop on advance request. The company operating the MV Lady Rose also rents Coleman and Grumman canoes at reasonable rates.

An alternate means of getting to Ucluelet or back to Port Alberni is to take the bus operated by Orient Stage Lines year round. The bus route continues along the entire length of Long Beach as far as Tofino.

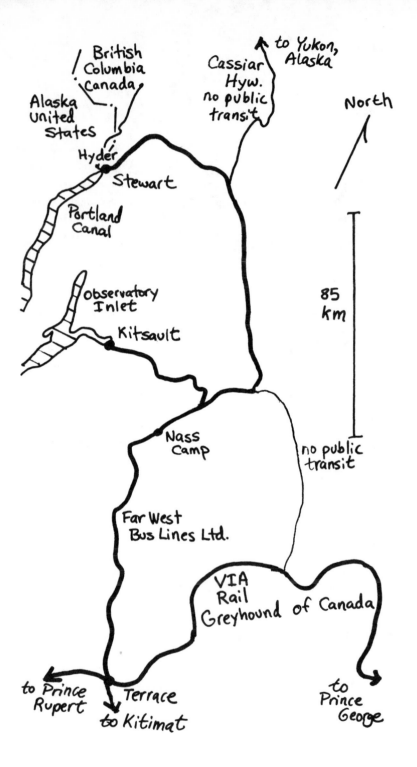

PORTLAND CANAL

Five kilometers from the Alaskan border, at the head of the Portland Canal ocean inlet, the town of Stewart, British Columbia is in the center of a dramatic area of icefields, fjords, thick forests and steep walled mountains. There are few trails and other formal amenities, but this remote area north of Prince Rupert is likely to attract a growing number of visitors.

Farwest Bus Lines provides service to Stewart from Terrace and Kitimat twice weekly. Terrace is on the main Yellowhead Highway between Jasper and Prince Rupert and can be reached on VIA Rail, Greyhound of Canada and several airlines. Both Kitimat and Stewart are served by Trans-Provincial Airlines. Prince Rupert, the major community in this part of British Columbia, can be reached by British Columbia Ferries, the Alaska Marine Highway System, several airlines, Greyhound of Canada and VIA Rail.

There are at least two trails that can be used as a starting point for exploring the area. The United Empire Trail starts at the water tank on the north end of Stewart, just before the bridge crossing the Bear River. After a several hour, uphill hike, the trail reaches the abandoned United Empire Mine, passing old buildings and mine workings along the way. The Barney Gulch Trail starts from the left side of the road leading to the Stewart dump. This road is located just north of the Bear River Bridge on the opposite side of the road as the water tank.

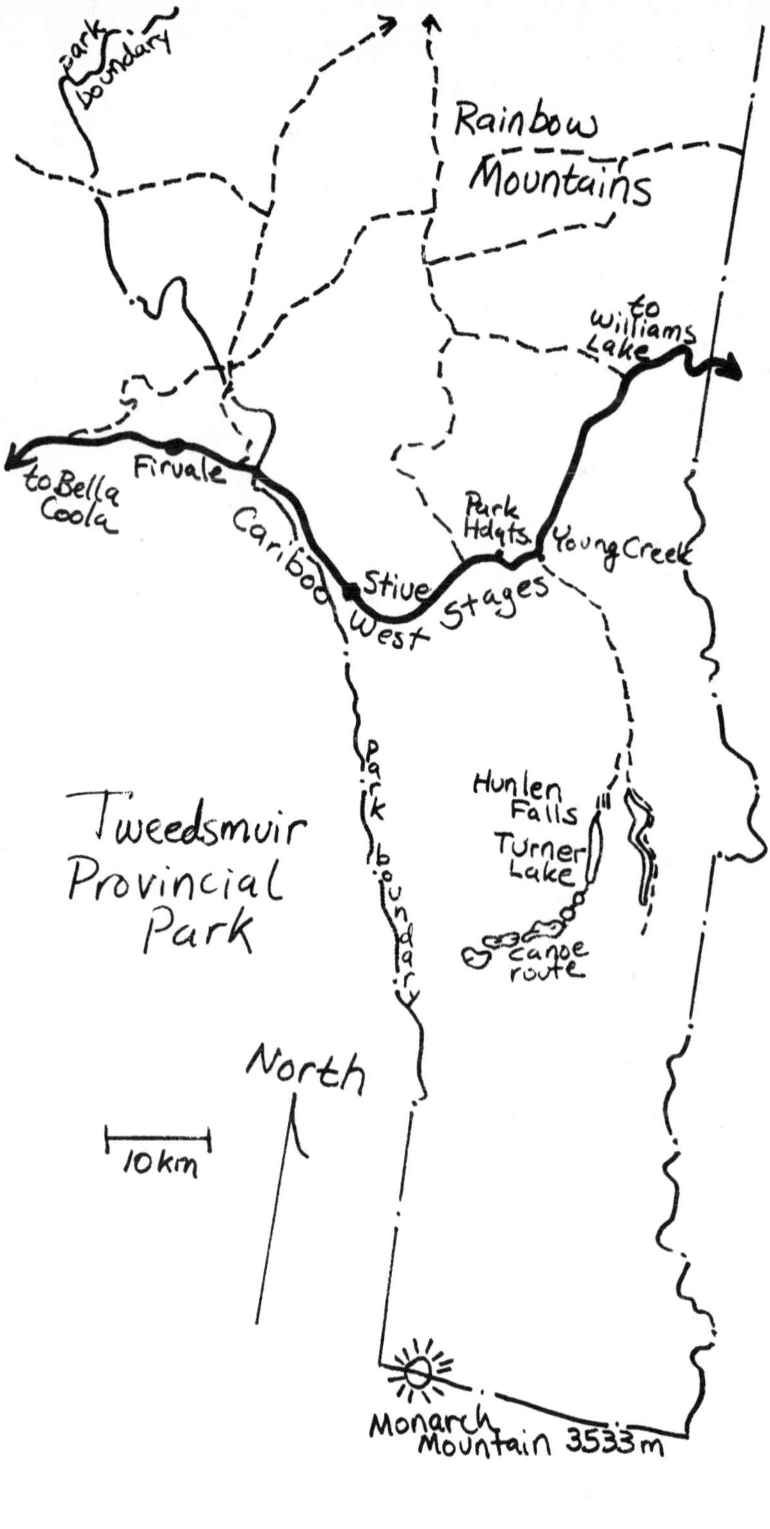

park boundary

Rainbow Mountains

to williams Lake

Firvale

to Bella Coola

Cariboo

Park Hdqts

Young Creek

Stuie

West Stages

Park boundary

Hunlen Falls

Turner Lake

canoe route

Tweedsmuir Provincial Park

North

10km

Monarch Mountain 3533m

TWEEDSMUIR PROVINCIAL PARK

Tweedsmuir is a remote central British Columbia park on the scale of Yellowstone and Denali. Within the one million hectares are peaks of 3500 meters, meadows, glaciers, bears, caribou, mountain goats, moose and wolves.

British Columbia Highway 20 traverses the park and is the only public transportation corridor. Cariboo West Stages has two roundtrips weekly between Bella Coola and Williams Lake. On the bus route west towards Bella Coola, several trailheads are passed, although only the stop at Firvale is within five km of a trail. This route leads north along the route of Alexander MacKenzie, who traveled through this area in 1793. The one scheduled stop within the park boundaries is at Stiue, which has good salmon fishing in season.

Contact Cariboo West Stages to arrange stops at other points within the park, including trailheads into the Rainbow Mountains, a scenic alpine area, and the Hunlen Falls Trail, which starts at Young Creek Picnic Ground. In addition to the spectacular namesake 260 meter waterfall, this trail also provides access to a 19 km canoe trail along a chain of lakes draining into the Atnarko River. Canoes can be rented from Hunlen Wilderness Camp (Box 308, Bella Coola, B.C. V0T 1C0), located on Turner Lake at the start of the trail.

Williams Lake can be reached by Greyhound of Canada and the British Columbia Railway, both from Vancouver. There is no public transportation available to Bella Coola other than a couple small airlines and Cariboo West Stages.

Yoho National Park

Banff National Park

Yoho Pass

to Vancouver

Wapta

Lake O'Hara Lodge

Lake Louise

Field

Lake O'Hara

to Banff Calgary

Greyhound Golden

VIA RAIL

West Gate

Kootenay National Park

North

10 km

YOHO NATIONAL PARK

Directly west of Banff National Park in one of the most scenic areas of the Canadian Rockies, Yoho is an excellent hiker's park with 420 km of trail, the best of it accessible using public transportation.

Greyhound of Canada, on its Vancouver to Calgary route, stops, or will make flag stops, several times daily in each direction at West Gate, Field Junction and Wapta Lodge. VIA Rail stops daily in Field, the park headquarters. Lake O'Hara Lodge operates a shuttle bus daily in the summer from Lake Louis Junction (Greyhound and VIA Rail stops) into the Lake O'Hara area, where several days to a week could be spent on a network of trails. Lake O'Hara is also an excellent area for ski touring and snowshoeing in season. Reservations are required for the Lake O'Hara shuttle service and can be made by calling Yoho National Park at (604) 343-6324.

The other center for hiking is in the Yoho Valley area, accessible by backpacking over Burgess and Yolo Passes from Field.

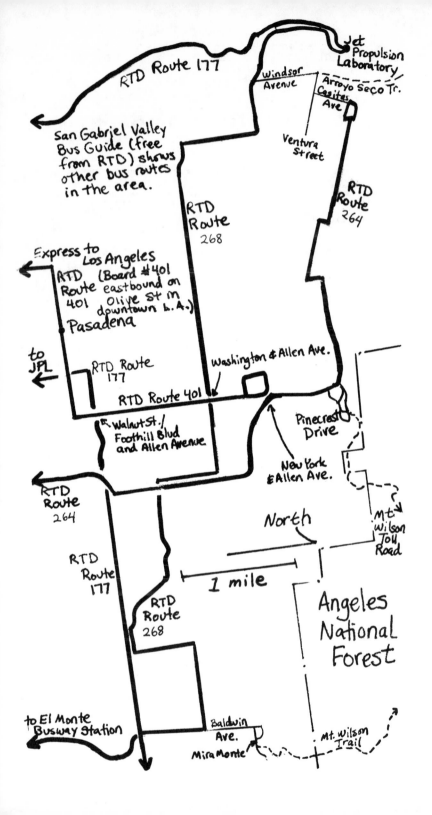

ANGELES NATIONAL FOREST

The city of Los Angeles sprawls at the foot of the Angeles National Forest and the Southern California Rapid Transit District (RTD) provides bus service that reaches almost to the forest boundary. Within the Angeles Forest are the jumbled mountains and canyons separating Los Angeles from the high desert.

RTD routes 268 and 177 serve Jet Propulsion Laboratory (JPL) from downtown Pasadena, weekdays only. Route 401 provides freeway express service from downtown Los Angeles to Pasadena. Near the entrance of JPL, at the corner of Ventura Street and Windsor Avenue, is a road that becomes the trail up the canyon of the Arroyo Seco, one of the largest streams in southern California. A hike up the old Mt. Wilson Toll Road, now closed to traffic, and then into spring fed Eaton Canyon, is possible by taking Route 264 (weekdays only) to the corner of Altadena Drive and Allen Avenue. A short distance east on Altadena Drive, on the east loop of Pinecrest Drive, is the start of the hike. This area is closed during high fire danger, usually from June until the first winter rains.

There are a few other possibilities, including visits on weekends, although greater distances are required to reach the trailheads from bus stops. Write the RTD for their San Gabriel Valley Bus Guide (free) and match up the north end of bus routes with trailheads on an Angeles National Forest map.

Also of interest for L.A. visitors is Route 431 from Santa Monica to north Los Angeles County beaches. Leo Carrillo State Beach at the end of the route has beach and canyon camping (reservations required) as well as some day hiking. The inland backdrop for much of this route is the Santa Monica Mountains National Recreation Area, which when fully developed will have some overnight hiking opportunities.

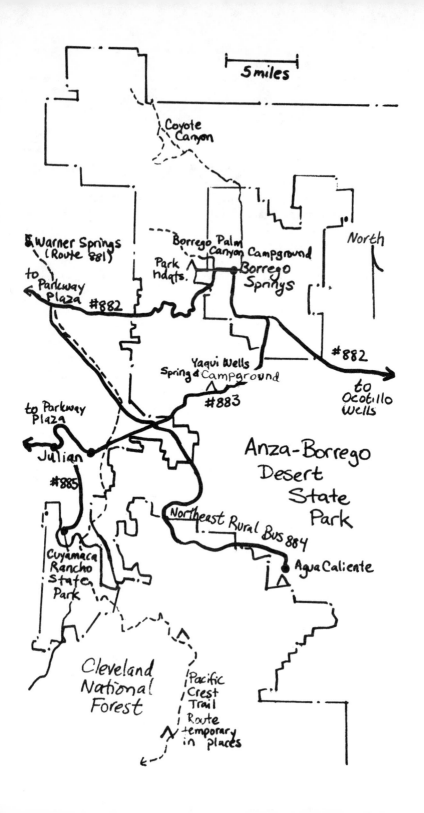

ANZA - BORREGO DESERT STATE PARK

California's largest state park has many varied possibilities for hiking in its half-million acres of desert terrain.
Desert bighorn are found here and California fan palms
grow around natural seeps and springs.

The Northeast Rural Bus System provides service four
times weekly to Borrego Springs in the center of the
park from the San Diego area (Routes 882 and 883). Route
882 is a once weekly extension to Ocotillo Wells in the
eastern part of the park. The nearby Cleveland National
Forest and Cuyamaca Rancho State Park also offer hiking
opportunities, but the infrequent twice monthly service
to Lake Cuyamaca (Route 885) will make visits impractical
for most hikers. Routes 881, 882, 883, 884 and 885 all
provide access to the Pacific Crest Trail, which traverses
the western edge of Anza-Borrego Park. All Northeast
Rural Buses leave from Parkway Plaza, El Cajon, a San
Diego suburb. Connections can be made there for public
transit to and from San Diego. All of the Northeast Rural
Buses will make flag stops and reservations can also
be made at least 24 hours in advance [phone: (619) 765-
0145]. In addition, these buses are equipped with bicycle
racks capable of holding two bicycles.

There are a variety of backpacking trips that can be
undertaken in Anza-Borrego, some along maintained trails,
others on jeep roads, and elsewhere cross-country. The
park headquarters, about three miles outside Borrego
Springs, can provide more detailed information. Close
by is the Palm Canyon Campground and a trail leading
past the Borrego Palm Canyon oasis.

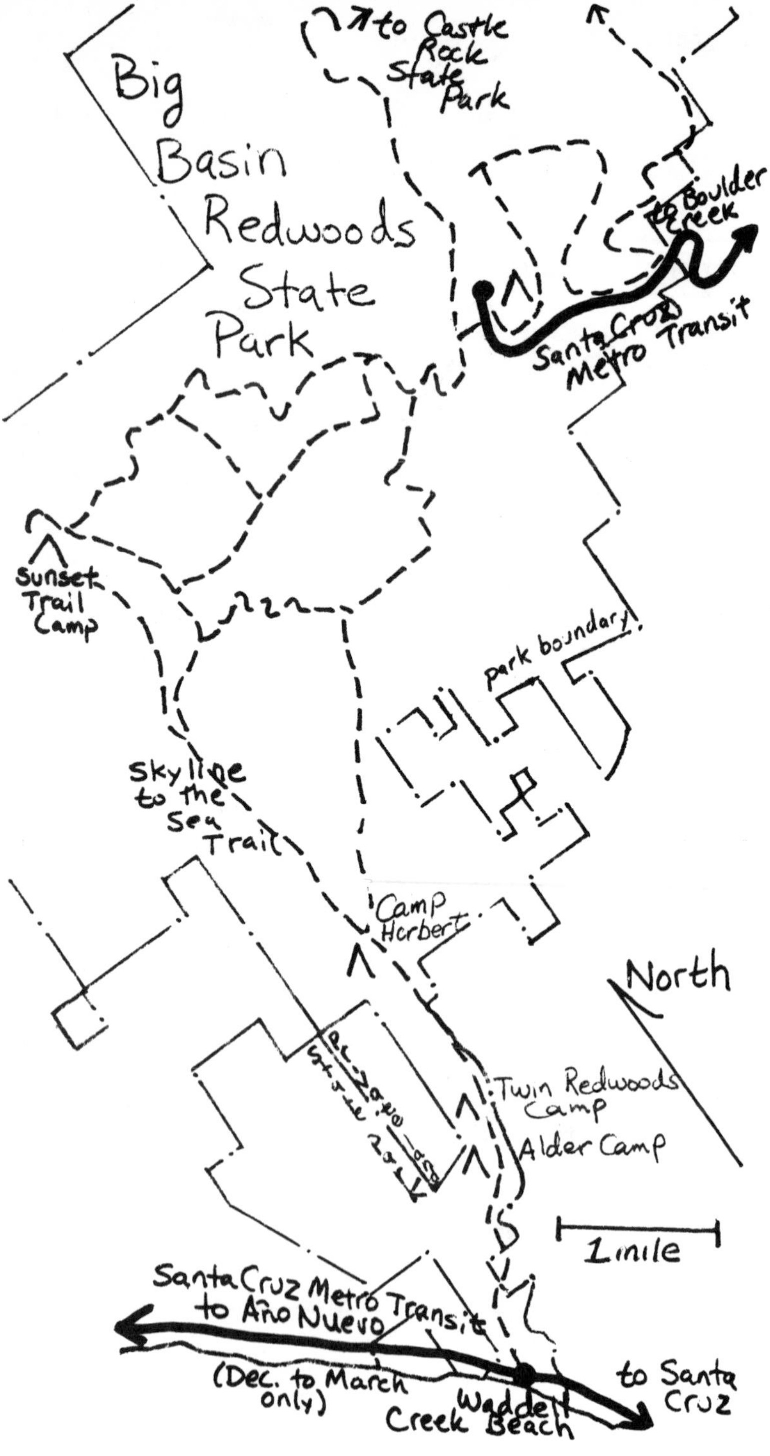

Big
Basin
Redwoods
State
Park

to Castle
Rock
State
Park

to Boulder
Creek

Santa Cruz
Metro Transit

Sunset
Trail
Camp

park boundary

Skyline
to the
Sea
Trail

Camp
Herbert

North

Twin Redwoods
Camp

Alder Camp

1 mile

Santa Cruz Metro Transit
to Año Nuevo

(Dec. to March
only)

Waddell
Creek Beach

to Santa
Cruz

BIG BASIN REDWOODS STATE PARK

Big Basin Redwoods is one of California's oldest and largest state parks and includes some of the last old growth redwoods south of San Francisco. There is a large network of trails for day hiking and one major backpacking trip. The Skyline to the Sea Trail starts in Castle Rock State Park at the crest of the Santa Cruz Mountains (inaccessible using public transportation), passes through Big Basin and terminates at Waddell Creek Beach. Contact Big Basin Park administrative offices beforehand for trail camp reservations.

Santa Cruz Metropolitan Transit District provides service to both Big Basin and to Waddell Creek daily. Service is twice daily to Big Basin via Routes 35 and 37 and several times daily to Waddell Creek via Route 40. Routes 35 and 40 depart from the Santa Cruz Metro Center, adjacent to the Greyhound and Peerless Stages depot. For access to Big Basin, transfer from the Route 35 to the Route 37 in Boulder Creek. Greyhound serves Santa Cruz from San Francisco (including the Airport) and Monterey-Salinas (AMTRAK). Service from Oakland, the San Jose Airport and San Jose is via Peerless Stages. AMTRAK serves San Jose.

There are several other state parks in the Santa Cruz area that are accessible using Santa Cruz buses, although for the most part, hiking is limited to day excursions. Route 30 serves a campground in Henry Cowell Redwoods State Park, a 4000 acre wooded area on the banks of the San Lorenzo River. Fall Creek State Park is roughly between Routes 35 and 41 just north of Felton Empire Road. Wilder Ranch State Park is located four miles north of Santa Cruz, just off Route 40. Both of these parks are undeveloped. Finally, between December and March, call the Santa Cruz bus system for information on bus access for tours of the Año Nuevo State Reserve elephant seal rookery, which is just north of Waddell Creek and served by Route 40.

Los Angeles

Avalon
(ferry)

Interior Swade

Catalina

Black Jack
Campground

Airport

Two Harbors

ferry

Campground

Little Harbor
Campground

Parsons
Landing

Catalina
Island

North

2 miles

CATALINA ISLAND

Though Catalina Island is almost entirely owned by the Wrigley's chewing gum interests, an innovative open space easement arranged with Los Angeles County essentially has made the island the country's largest county park: 41,000 acres of largely unspoiled southern California landscape. Access to the island is the easiest of any of southern California's islands.

Catalina can be reached from Long Beach (Catalina Cruises), San Pedro (Catalina Cruises and Catalina Express) and Newport Beach, summer only (Catalina Passenger Service). Reservations are required for all sailings, most of which serve Avalon on the east end of the island. Two Harbors is the other island port that there is scheduled service to. On the mainland, the Long Beach terminal is most easily reached on public buses. Call the Southern California Rapid Transit District (213) 626-4455 or Long Beach Transit (213) 591-2301 for current schedules. It is also possible to fly to the island; check with a travel agent for the current carriers.

Once on the island, the Catalina Island Interior Shuttle Bus provides transportation along 23 miles of road. Reservations are required. Permits are necessary to hike on the trails, jeep roads and surfaced roads and can be obtained from the Santa Catalina Island Conservancy (address in Appendix II). Reservations are required to use the two campgrounds operated by the Los Angeles County Department of Parks and Recreation at Little Harbor and Black Jack. Parsons Landing and Little Fisherman's Cove Campsites are operated by the Cove and Camp Agency and the Santa Catalina Island Co. operates a campground just outside of Avalon. Check Appendix II for addresses and phone numbers.

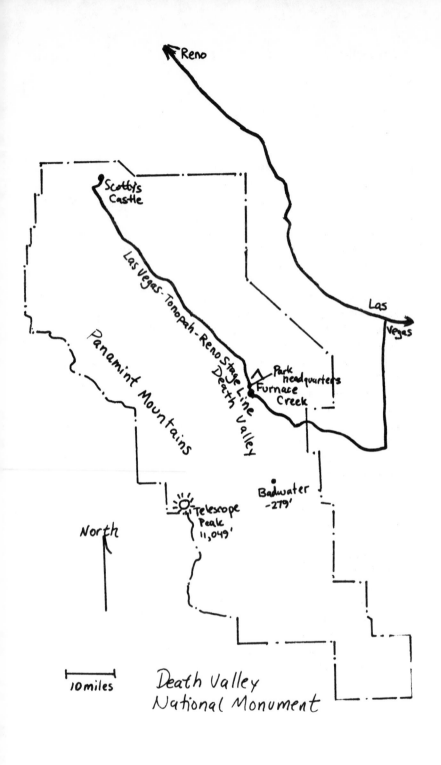

Reno

Scotty's Castle

Las Vegas-Tonopah-Reno Stage Line

Death Valley

Panamint Mountains

Park headquarters

Furnace Creek

Las Vegas

Badwater -279'

Telescope Peak 11,049'

North

10 miles

Death Valley National Monument

DEATH VALLEY NATIONAL MONUMENT

Death Valley sprawls over a wide variety of California and Nevada desert terrain. There are many opportunities for hiking and desert appreciation, although the park is short on the designated trails and routes that backpackers may be accustomed to. Hiking on jeep roads and following dry washes up into the surrounding mountains are some of the possible trips.

The Las Vegas-Tonopah-Reno Stage Line provides service from Las Vegas to Furnace Creek and Scotty's Castle, November 1 to March 1, two to five times per week.

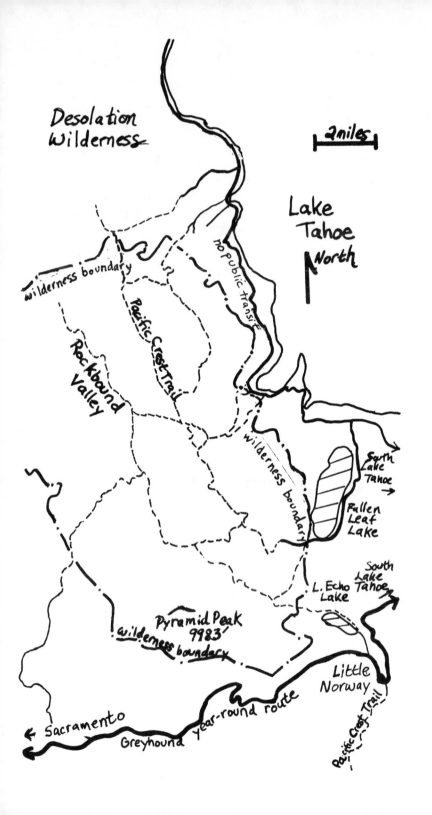

Desolation
Wilderness

2 miles

Lake
Tahoe

North

no public transit

wilderness boundary

Pacific Crest Trail

Rockbound
Valley

wilderness boundary

South
Lake
Tahoe

Fallen
Leaf
Lake

South
Lake
Tahoe

L. Echo
Lake

Pyramid Peak
9983

wilderness boundary

Little
Norway

Sacramento

Greyhound year-round route

Pacific Crest Trail

DESOLATION WILDERNESS

The 63,469 acre Desolation Wilderness contains the best
hiking, ski touring and snowshoeing opportunities in
the Lake Tahoe Basin. Permits are required and can be
obtained through the El Dorado National Forest. Much
of the wilderness is studded with small lakes and there
is an extensive trail system.

Greyhound has year round daily service to South Lake
Tahoe from Sacramento. The once daily local bus will
stop on request at Little Norway, near Echo Summit. From
this area, an unpaved road, suitable for crosscountry
skiing in winter, leads past vacation cabins with views
of Lake Tahoe to the edge of the wilderness at Echo Lakes.
The Pacific Crest Trail enters the wilderness at this
point.

In addition to Greyhound service from Sacramento and Reno,
it is also possible to get to South Lake Tahoe from Reno
via Las Vegas-Tonopah-Reno Stage Line. This several times
daily bus also serves Reno International Airport. Both
Reno and Sacramento are served by AMTRAK and Trailways
in addition to Greyhound.

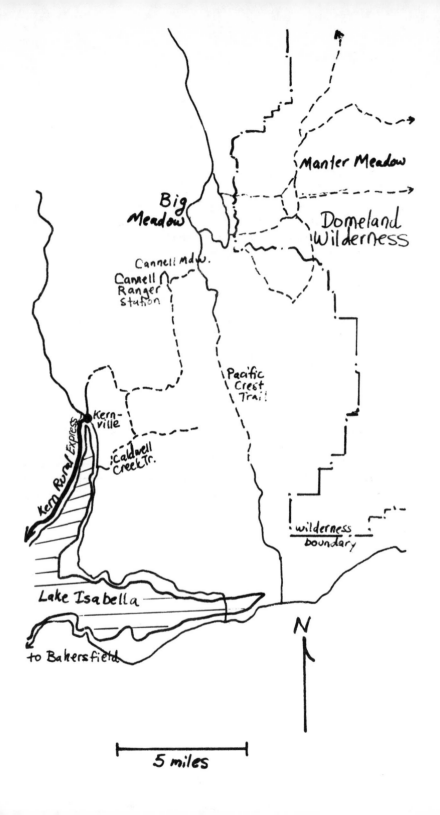

Manter Meadow

Big
Meadow

Domeland
Wilderness

Cannell Mdw.

Cannell
Ranger
Station

Pacific
Crest
Trail

Kern
ville

Kern Rural Express

Caldwell
Creek Tr.

wilderness
boundary

Lake Isabella

to Bakersfield

N

5 miles

DOMELAND WILDERNESS

The Domeland Wilderness is closer to Los Angeles than any other Sierra wilderness, but it is curiously unknown compared to the overcrowded high country to the north. Sagebrush and piñon pine are the dominant vegetation and elevations reach 9000 feet.

Six days weekly year round, Kern Rural Transit Systems provides service to Kernville from Bakersfield. Nearby are both the Pacific Crest Trail and the Caldwell Creek Trail. Both trails enter the wilderness after crossing an unpaved road at Cannell Meadow. Also nearby is the largest single subalpine meadow in California, appropriately though not imaginatively named, Big Meadow.

Bakersfield is served by Greyhound, Trailways, AMTRAK and several airlines. Golden Empire Transit provides local transportation.

EMIGRANT WILDERNESS

Just to the north of Yosemite, the Emigrant Wilderness is relatively uncrowded by California standards. A thickly forested area, dotted with numerous lakes and crowned by several 10,000 foot peaks, it has a network of trails accessible from the Greyhound bus stop at Pinecrest, which has service only during the summer. Walking east on Stanislaus National Forest roads 4N34, 4N26 or 4N02Y leads to several trails into the wilderness. Also at Pinecrest are several forest service campgrounds and a ranger station.

Greyhound service to Pinecrest is provided via the Gold Rush town of Sonora from the Stockton Greyhound station. Stockton has major airline service, and AMTRAK and Trailways in addition to Greyhound service.

Aquilegia truncata

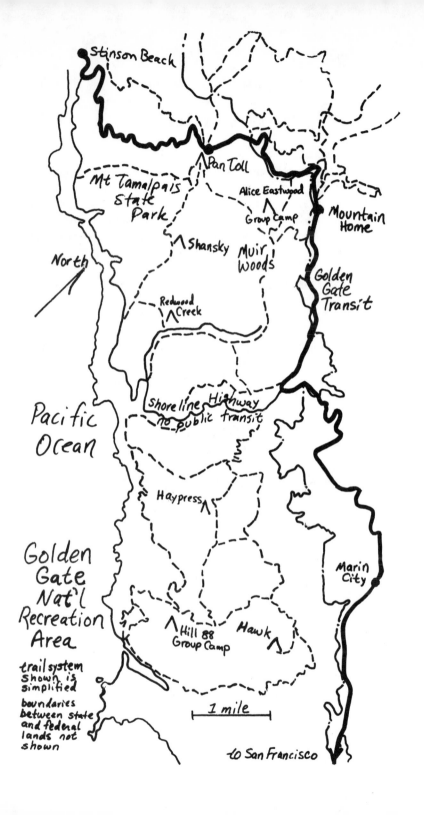

GOLDEN GATE NATIONAL RECREATION AREA

The Golden Gate Recreation Area is part of a new concept in national park management: to bring parks to people by protecting urban open space. The park extends from playgrounds in San Francisco to the wilder coastline at Point Reyes. It includes surplus military lands, Muir Woods National Monument and several state parks.

Bus service is most frequent during the summer and on weekends and holidays. Golden Gate Transit has several routes reaching into the area, including Route 63, which provides a number of roundtrips to Mt. Tamalpais State Park on weekends and holidays. A network of trails start from the stop at Mountain Home Inn. The Pan Toll stop has camping available nearby on a first-come, first-served basis. On weekdays, commuter hour service is provided by Route 61.

Route 61 originates at the Sausalito ferry terminal and passes through Marin City enroute to Mt. Tamalpais. Route 63 originates in Marin City. To reach Marin City from the San Francisco Greyhound depot, walk one block to 7th and Market to board buses to Marin City (as of this writing, Routes 10, 20 and 50). For ferry departures to Marin County, the San Francisco ferry terminal is located at the base of Market Street on San Francisco Bay, a long walk from Greyhound. Using the Bay Area Rapid Transit subway from 7th and Market to Embarcadero Station will put you within easy walking distance of the ferry terminal. AMTRAK connecting buses from Oakland will leave you off at the Transbay Terminal, next to Trailways. From the entrance of either terminal, walk north two blocks to Market Street, turn right and descend about five blocks to the ferry terminal.

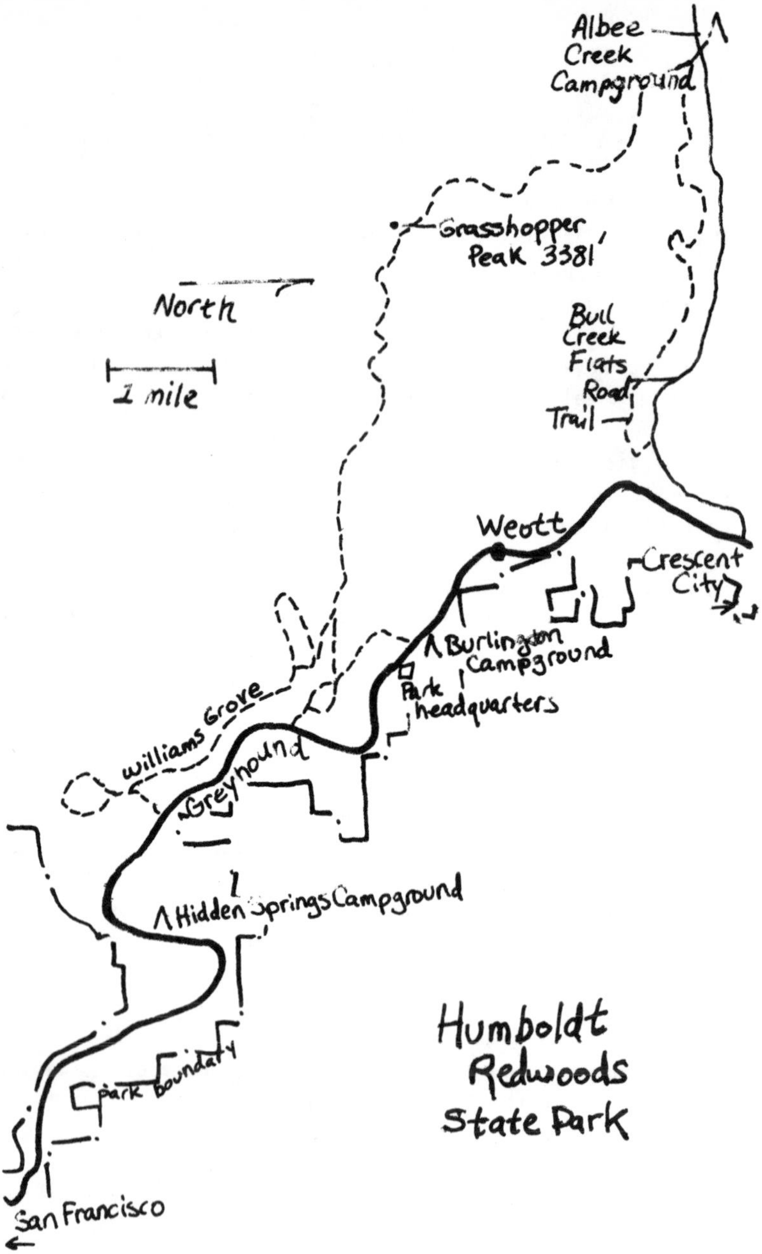

Albee
Creek
Campground

Grasshopper
Peak 3381'

North

1 mile

Bull
Creek
Flats
Road
Trail

Weott

Crescent
City

Burlington
Campground

Williams Grove

Park
headquarters

Greyhound

Hidden Springs Campground

Humboldt
Redwoods
State Park

Park boundary

San Francisco

HUMBOLDT REDWOODS STATE PARK

One of California's larger state parks with 43,000 acres, Humboldt Redwoods protects a number of fine redwood groves as well as thousands of acres of upland watershed.

Greyhound makes several stops daily in each direction at Weott on its San Francisco to Eureka route. The Williams Grove and Grasshopper Peak trails are nearby, as is the park headquarters and Burlington Campground. Hiking is probably best from June to September because at other times, high river crossings can limit access. All designated campgrounds are close to roads, so backpacking opportunities are limited on the thirty-six miles of trail.

JOHN MUIR WILDERNESS

A 500,000 acre alpine wilderness along the eastern Sierra crest, the John Muir Wilderness adjoins Sequoia and Kings Canyon National Parks. Together these protected lands constitute one of the largest wildernesses in the United States. Permits are required prior to entering the area. Write the Inyo National Forest for information on entry limits and backcountry restrictions.

Greyhound, on its once daily Reno to Los Angeles route, serves the Eastern Sierra towns of Mammoth Lakes, Bishop, Big Pine, Independence and Lone Pine, but this still leaves fifteen to twenty miles and several thousand feet elevation gain to reach most trailheads. From June through September, The Outdoorsman operates a shuttle bus twice daily from Bishop to Lake Sabrina and South Lake. The bus stop in Bishop is behind City Hall. The National Park Service and the Forest Service also have a frequent daily shuttle bus from Mammoth Lakes into the Reds Meadow-Devil's Postpile area, but only during the summer. Winter service to the Mammoth Mountain Chalet from Bishop is available several days per week on another Outdoorsman shuttle. Another potential winter trip would involve getting off Greyhound at the Rock Creek flag stop between Bishop and Mammoth Lakes and crosscountry skiing up the unplowed Rock Creek Road eleven miles to the wilderness boundary.

Two other firms, Eastern Sierra Shuttle and High Sierra Stages, will provide transportation to and from many Sierra trailheads on an advanced reservation basis, but neither operates on a fixed schedule. Eastern Sierra Shuttle is based in Lone Pine and serves a number of trailheads in southern Owens Valley, including Mt. Whitney. High Sierra Stages is based in Visalia, on the west side of the Sierra, convenient for cross-mountain trips.

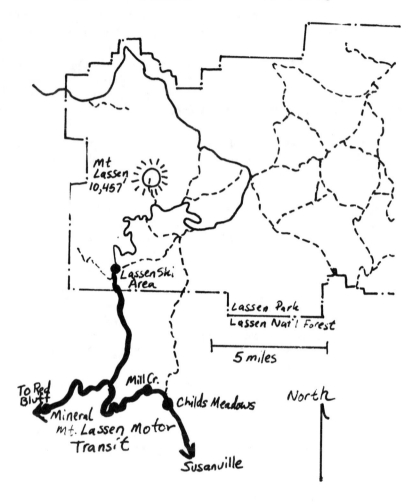

Lassen Volcanic National Park

Mt Lassen 10,457'

Lassen Ski Area

Lassen Park
Lassen Nat'l Forest

5 miles

To Red Bluff

Mill Cr.

Childs Meadows

Mineral
Mt. Lassen Motor Transit

Susanville

North

LASSEN VOLCANIC NATIONAL PARK

Until Mt. St. Helens erupted, Mt. Lassen, the southern most Cascade volcano, was the only peak to erupt in this century in the contiguous United States. During the winter months from November to April, when the Lassen Ski Area is open, there is on-call service available to the ski area at the southwest corner of the park. This bus service, on Wednesdays through Sundays, can be arranged by contacting Mt. Lassen Motor Transit, which serves the park from Red Bluff and Susanville. There are good ski touring and snowshoeing opportunities near the ski area although avalanche danger can be high.

Year round, Mt. Lassen Motor Transit will make a flag stop at Childs Meadow in Lassen National Forest. From here a trail leads north into the park and interconnects with several other trails. In theory it is possible to obtain the required wilderness permit at Lassen Park headquarters in Mineral. The eastbound bus towards Susanville makes a half-hour stop there before proceeding past Childs Meadow. The park will also issue permits by mail and that is the recommended approach for public transportation. users.

Red Bluff can be reached by either Greyhound or Trailways. The nearest AMTRAK station is in Redding. Susanville is served by the Greyhound system.

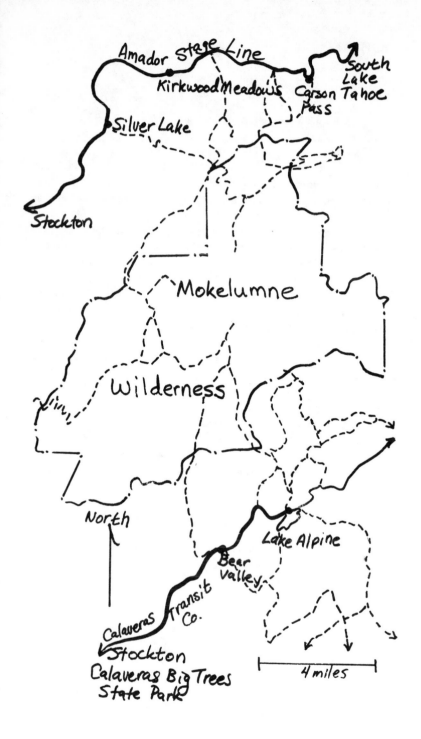

Amador State Line

Kirkwood Meadows

South Lake Tahoe

Carson Pass

Silver Lake

Stockton

Mokelumne

Wilderness

North

Lake Alpine

Bear Valley

Calaveras Transit Co.

Stockton
Calaveras Big Trees
State Park

4 miles

MOKELUMNE WILDERNESS

A 50,165 acre area, the Mokelumne Wilderness protects
a glaciated section of the northern Sierra.

Amador Stage Line provides service several times weekly
from Stockton to South Lake Tahoe, with the stops at Silver
Lake, Kirkwood Meadows and Carson Pass having trails into
the wilderness. To reach trailheads on the south side
of the wilderness, the Calaveras Transit Company bus from
Stockton can be used to get to Lake Alpine. Service to
Lake Alpine and to the Sequoia grove at Calaveras Big
Trees State Park is on an on-call basis one day per week,
so call ahead to make arrangements.

Stockton is served by Greyhound, Trailways, AMTRAK and
several airlines. The Stockton Metropolitan Transit District
provides local transportation.

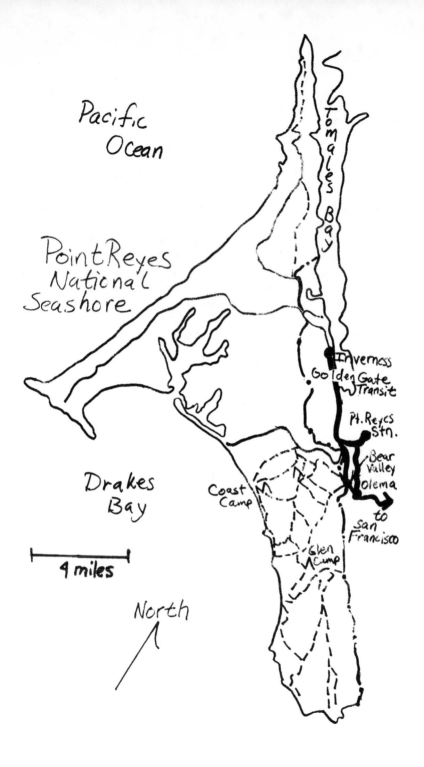

Pacific
Ocean

PointReyes
National
Seashore

Tomales Bay

Inverness
Golden Gate Transit

Pt. Reyes Stn.

Bear Valley
Olema

Drakes
Bay

Coast Camp

to san Francisco

Glen Camp

4 miles

North

POINT REYES NATIONAL SEASHORE

Isolated from the rest of the northern California coast by the San Andreas Fault, the Point Reyes Peninsula is an unpopulated anamoly along the crowded California coast. Nevertheless this is a popular park and advance reservations are required to use the campsites in Bear Valley, the major backpacking area in the park.

Golden Gate Transit Route 64 provides two round trips per day on weekends and holidays from San Francisco to the Bear Valley trailheads near the National Park Service headquarters. The bus leaves from the San Francisco Zoo and also stops enroute in Marin City. See the Golden Gate National Recreation Area description for information on how to get to Marin City from various public transportation terminals in San Francisco. After Marin City, Route 64 also stops at Samuel P. Taylor State Park, a redwood forested area with primitive camping available for hikers and bicyclists (reservations required).

Weekday service to Point Reyes is via Route 65, which operates once a day in early morning (southbound) and late evening (northbound). No service is provided to the Bear Valley trailheads, but the stop in Olema is a few minutes walk away. Unlike the weekend bus, a transfer is necessary to get to San Francisco. Get off at San Anselmo, where a number of buses can be used to get back to San Francisco.

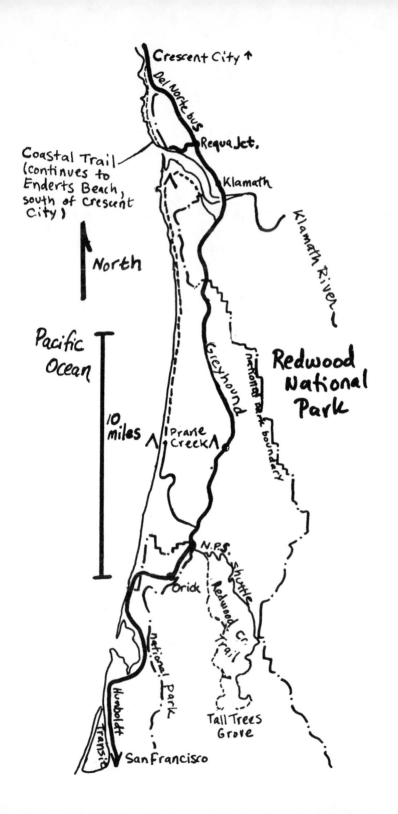

Crescent City ↑

Del Norte bus

Requa Jct.

Klamath

Klamath River

Coastal Trail (continues to Enderts Beach, south of Crescent City)

↑ North

Pacific Ocean

Redwood National Park

national park boundary

Greyhound

10 miles

Prarie Creek

N.P.S. shuttle

Orick

Redwood Cr. Trail

national Park

Tall Trees Grove

Humboldt Transit

San Francisco

REDWOOD NATIONAL PARK

The towering giants of northern California give the stream-
side canyons a vertical environment of their own. The
area has good day hiking, particularly in the well established California state parks that make up the base of
the park. The one major backpacking trip is the hike up
Redwood Creek, easily accessible in the low water summer
season only. Newly constructed sections of trail have
also created a unified coastal trail that follows the
shore of much of the park. The Greyhound flag stop at
Requa Junction provides access to the trail as well as
much of the Del Norte City and Public Bus route from Crescent
City to Klamath (twice daily except holidays).The Del Norte
bus directly serves Requa, providing closer access to
the shoreline. Three primitive campsites are available
along the coastal trail, spaced about a day's walk apart
from each other.

The Redwood Creek trailhead is about three miles from
Orick, a stop on Greyhound's Crescent City to San Francisco
route. It can be reached by taking the summer only National
Park Service shuttle which operates on the Bald Hills
Road. For those who may not have the time to hike the
entire eight miles along Redwood Creek from the Redwood
Creek trailhead, the shuttle service also provides access
to a shorter hike of three miles roundtrip that meets
the eight mile trail at the Tall Trees Grove, site of
the world's largest trees.

Another way to reach Orick is via Humboldt Transit from
the Humboldt-Arcata-Eureka area, which has major airline
service in addition to Greyhound.

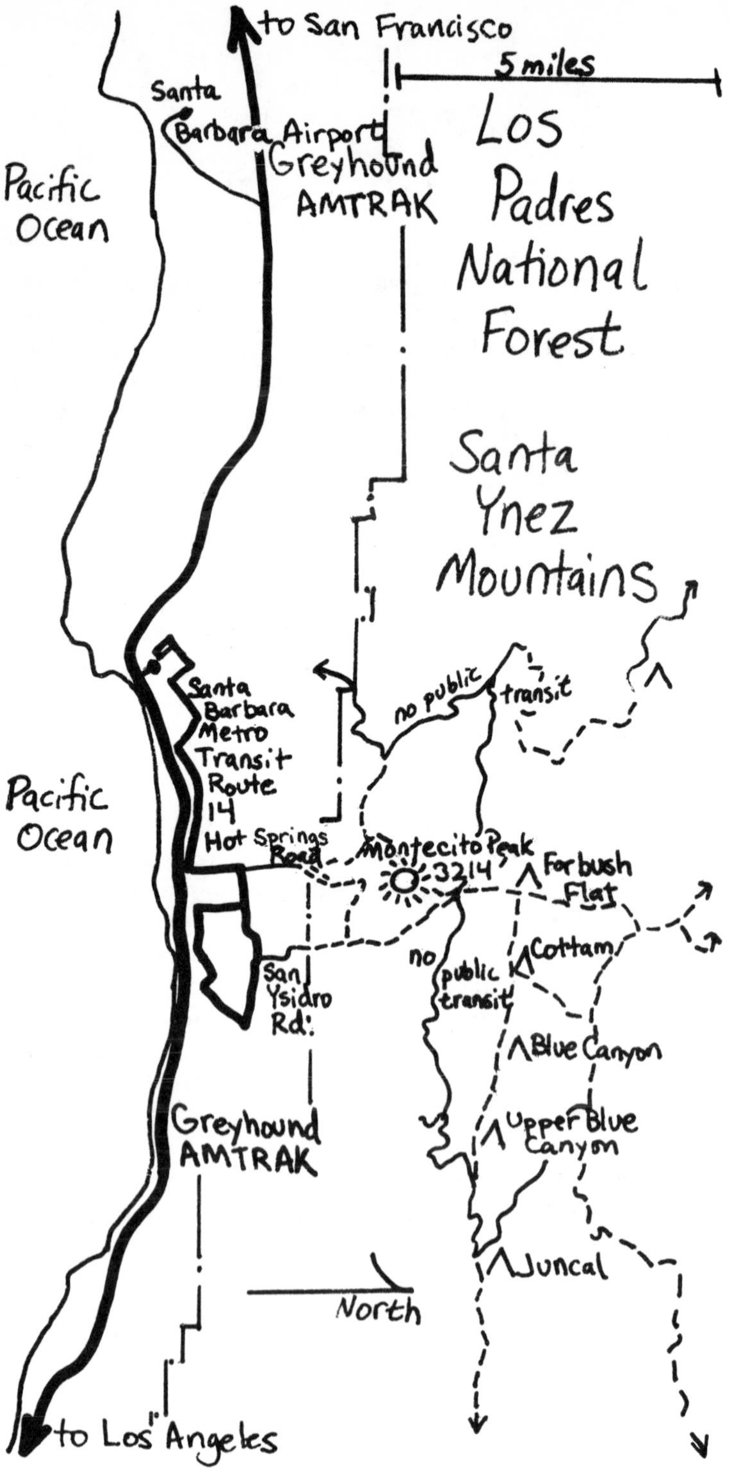

to San Francisco

5 miles

Santa
Barbara Airport
Greyhound
AMTRAK

Pacific
Ocean

LOS
Padres
National
Forest

Santa
Ynez
Mountains

no public transit

Santa
Barbara
Metro
Transit
Route
14

Pacific
Ocean

Hot Springs Road

Montecito Peak
3214

Forbush
Flat

San
Ysidro
Rd.

no public transit

Cottam

Blue Canyon

Greyhound
AMTRAK

Upper Blue
Canyon

Juncal

North

to Los Angeles

SANTA YNEZ MOUNTAINS

The Santa Ynez Mountains are one of a handful of mountain ranges in North America that run in an east to west direction, the consequence of intense faulting and earthquake stress in these chaparral covered mountains. The best hiking in the Los Padres National Forest is further away from Santa Barbara than the ridgelines that form a backdrop for the city.

Nevertheless, Santa Barbara Metropolitan Transit District Route 14 skirts the edge of the forest and presents a couple of possibilities. Hot Springs Canyon can be reached by getting off the Route 14 bus at East Valley Road and Hot Springs Road and walking north on Hot Springs Road about a mile until it becomes an unpaved fire road leading inside the national forest boundary. A trail past 3214 foot Montecito Peak leads over the crest of the mountains to camping areas at Forbush Flats, Cottam and Blue Canyon. Also in Hot Springs Canyon are the remains of a resort that centered around the canyon's thermal pools. It is also possible to walk over the crest of the Santa Ynez Mountains via San Ysidro Canyon, the next canyon east of Hot Springs Canyon. Get off the bus at San Ysidro and East Valley Roads and walk north on San Ysidro Road. Once again, hiking begins after a mile walk to the end of the paved road. The Route 14 bus runs six days per week on an approximately hourly basis during the day. The bus departs from the terminal at Chapala and Carrillo, adjacent to the Greyhound terminal. AMTRAK is located somewhat further away, but still within walking distance, at 209 State Street.

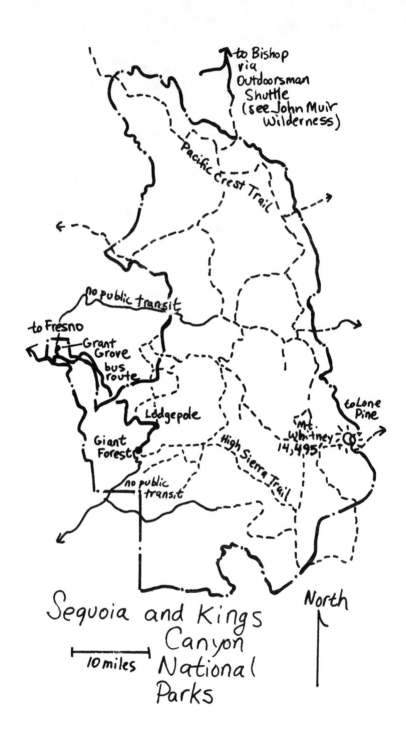

to Bishop via Outdoorsman Shuttle (see John Muir Wilderness)

Pacific Crest Trail

no public transit

to Fresno

Grant Grove bus route

Lodgepole

to Lone Pine

Giant Forest

Mt. Whitney 14,495'

High Sierra Trail

no public transit

Sequoia and Kings Canyon National Parks

10 miles

North

SEQUOIA AND KINGS CANYON NATIONAL PARKS

The largest tree, the highest mountain in the contiguous
United States and one of the deepest canyons make these
two adjoining parks a superlative area for hiking.

The Sequoia and Kings Canyon Hospitality Service provides
daily summer transportation to the parks from Fresno.
Stops are made in Fresno at Greyhound, AMTRAK and the
Fresno Air Terminal. Stops in the parks include Grant
Grove, Lodgepole and Giant Forest, which is the start
of the cross-mountain High Sierra Trail to Mt. Whitney.
Highlights of this trail include walking through giant
sequoia groves, climbing up to treeline at Kaweah Gap,
then past large wooded meadows and then down to almost
desert conditions at the bottom of the Kern River Canyon
before climbing high above treeline along the crest of
the Sierra at Mt. Whitney. There are numerous other possible
cross-Sierra trips taking a week or more. Consult the
John Muir Wilderness description for information on public
transportation on the east side of the mountains that can be
used to make these one-way trips possible.

Call the Sequoia and Kings Canyon Hospitality Service
ahead of time because bus reservations are required.

SISKIYOU MOUNTAINS

Close to the Oregon border, and spilling over the legal
boundary in places, the Siskiyous are one of several coastal
ranges that begin to take on the character of the Pacific
Northwest, draining moisture out of storms headed for
the drier valleys of California.

Siskiyou Transit and General Express operates two days
weekly from Yreka to Happy Camp in the Klamath National
Forest. Another route also served twice weekly provides
service as far as Etna. The area around Seiad Valley has
several trails, including the Pacific Crest Trail's last
major road crossing before reaching Oregon.

While it is not within the distance criteria set for the
book, it is possible to walk on unimproved roads to the
edge of the Marble Mountains Wilderness, the best hiking
area around the Siskiyous. The best stops would be at
Greenview, Etna or Happy Camp. The Pacific Crest Trail
also eventually enters the wilderness south of Seiad Valley.

Yreka can be reached on both Trailways and Greyhound.

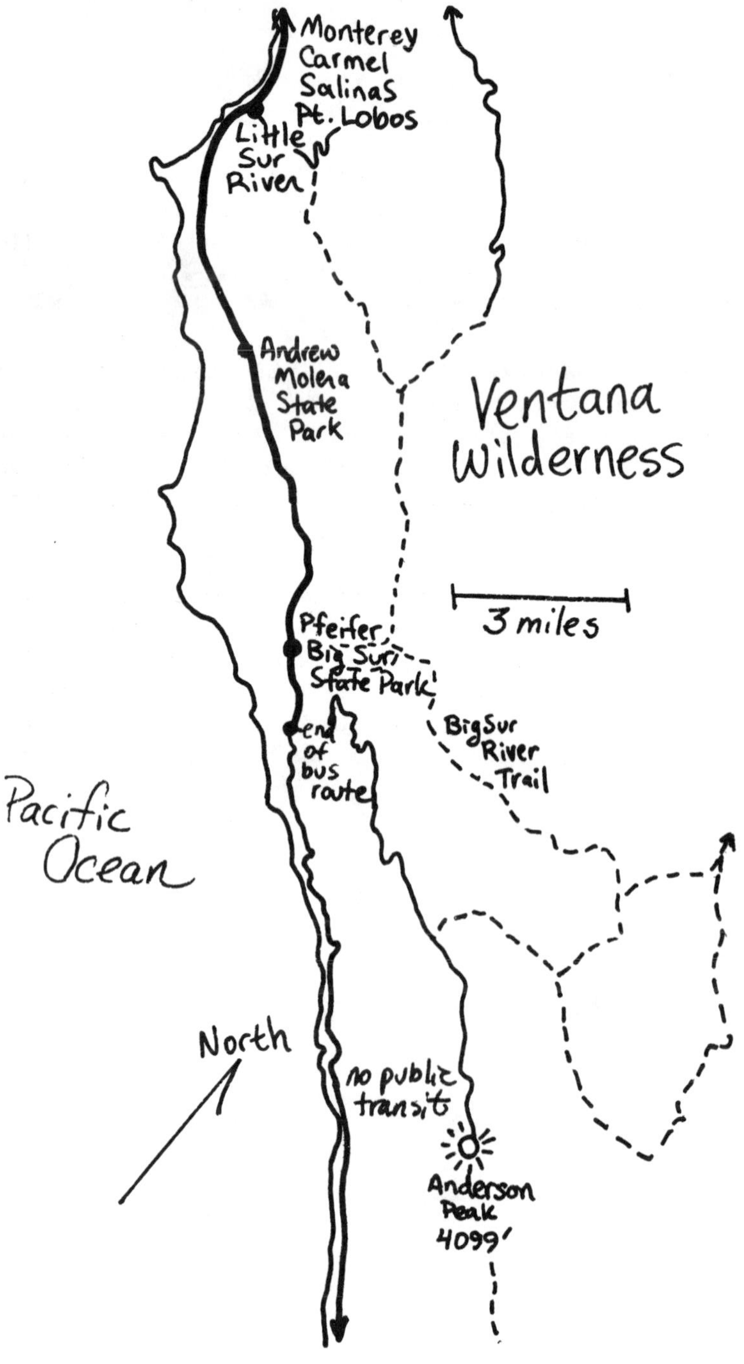

Monterey
Carmel
Salinas
Pt. Lobos

Little
Sur
River

Andrew
Molera
State
Park

Ventana
Wilderness

Pfeiffer
Big Sur
State Park

3 miles

end
of
bus
route

Big Sur
River
Trail

Pacific
Ocean

North

no public
transit

Anderson
Peak
4099'

VENTANA WILDERNESS

The Ventana Wilderness gives formal protection to the mountains that provide the backdrop for the Big Sur coast. The southern most redwoods grow in damp canyons, the rare Santa Lucia fir grows on chaparral covered hillsides and the poetry of Robinson Jeffers was inspired by the quiet beauty of these coastal mountains.

Monterey-Salinas Transit (MST) provides service to the Big Sur area via Route 22 daily from May through September, weekends only during the rest of the year. Route 22 leaves from the Monterey Transit Plaza, located at Pearl and Alvarado Streets. Greyhound's terminal is located on Del Monte Avenue, about six blocks away. The nearest AMTRAK station is in Salinas and MST Routes 20 and 21 can be used to get to Monterey from the Salinas Transit Center at Central Avenue and Salinas Street. AMTRAK and Greyhound are both several blocks from the Salinas Transit Center. Monterey Peninsula Airport is served by MST Route 21 on its scheduled run between Monterey and Salinas.

Once southbound on Route 22, stops can be made at a number of places including Andrew Molera State Park (beaches) and Point Lobos State Reserve (day use only). There is overnight camping available at Pfeiffer Big Sur State Park, which is adjacent to the Ventana Wilderness. A major trailhead into the wilderness is located just south of the park campground and it follows the canyon of the Big Sur River deep into the steep coastal mountains. Another trail climbs the ridgeline to the north of the Big Sur River, providing a spectacular view of the coastline below. There is also hiking available from the bus stop at the Coast Highway crossing of the Little Sur River.

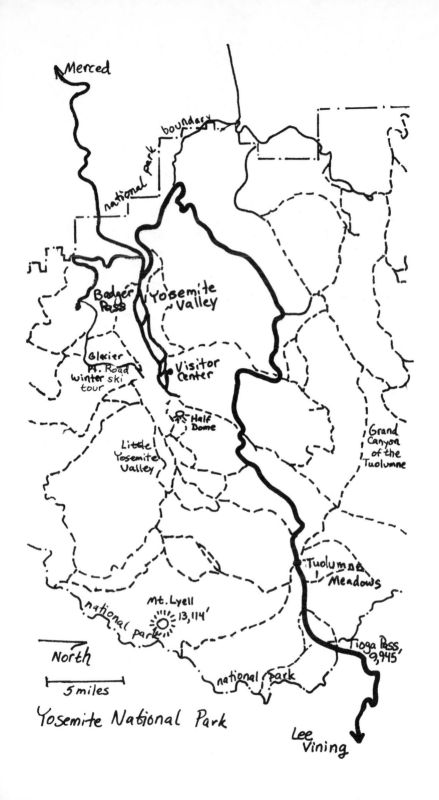

Merced

national park boundary

national park

Badger Pass

Yosemite Valley

Glacier Pt. Road winter ski tour

Visitor Center

Half Dome

Little Yosemite Valley

Grand Canyon of the Tuolumne

Tuolumne Meadows

Mt. Lyell 13,114'

national park

North

5 miles

national park

Tioga Pass 9,945'

Yosemite National Park

Lee Vining

YOSEMITE NATIONAL PARK

Yosemite is, of course, one of the best known national parks and is quite arguably, California's greatest scenic attraction. Bus service is available year round to the park from Merced. Direct connections with AMTRAK trains from the San Francisco Bay area are available at the Merced train station. The Yosemite Transportation System, which operates this bus, also operates a bus from Lee Vining in the summer. The Lee Vining-Yosemite Valley route is particularly of interest because it provides access to Tuolumne Meadows, a major center for hiking. Once in Yosemite Valley, the National Park Service operates free shuttle buses that provide access to trailheads within the valley. In the winter, one of these shuttle buses serves the Badger Pass ski area, which is also a popular jumping-off point for ski touring and snowshoeing.

Reservations for trips on the Yosemite Transportation System must be made at least 24 hours in advance and the National Park Service does have restrictions and quotas in effect governing backcountry use. In addition to AMTRAK, both Greyhound and Trailways reach Merced; Greyhound also has service to Lee Vining once daily in each direction on its Reno--Los Angeles route.

Uncompahgre
14,309'

Matterhorn
13,590'

Wetterhorn
14,015'

Big Blue
Wilderness

Grand Junction
Salt Lake

Ouray

no
public
transit

North

Trailways

2 miles

Red Mtn.

Telluride

Silverton
Albuquerque

BIG BLUE WILDERNESS

High alpine landscapes---in a history and scenery rich area make up the bulk of Big Blue Wilderness, created in 1980 from portions of the Uncompahgre Primitive Area. These mountains and the surrounding area have a long history of mining activity. Gold was discovered in 1873 and zinc, gold, lead and silver continue to be extracted.

The town of Ouray, on the once daily Albuquerque to Salt Lake City route of Trailways, is closest to the wilderness boundary to the east, as well as having hiking available to the west. Red Mountain, a flag stop between Ouray and Silverton to the south, also has hiking nearby, mostly on jeep roads, and there is no direct access into the Big Blue Wilderness.

The wilderness includes two 14,000 foot peaks; below timberline visitors will find forests of ponderosa pine, Englemann spruce, alpine fir and aspen. Wapiti, deer, bear and mountain sheep are also sometimes seen.

San Juan Mountains

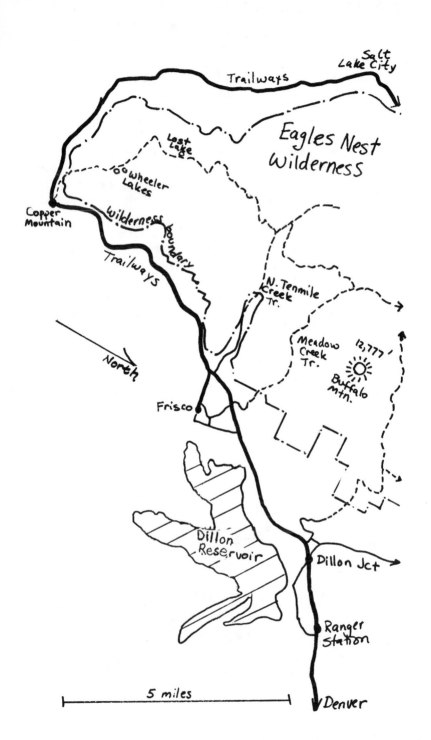

EAGLES NEST WILDERNESS

Beautiful alpine scenery is the setting for the Eagles Nest Wilderness in the mountains northeast of the Vail resort area.

Trailways, on its Denver-Salt Lake City route, serves Wheeler (Copper Mountain) once daily in each direction, but only to discharge passengers. Frisco is served with five round trips daily; it is a two mile walk from there to the trailhead on North Tenmile Creek. Dillon Junction, served with one round trip daily, also has a trail into the nearby wilderness, as well as an Arapaho National Forest ranger station.

Campanula rotundiflora

5 miles

to Denver

Minturn

Ranger
Station

Grouse
Lake

Turquoise
Lakes

Sawatch
Range

Holy
Cross
Wilderness

Mount of
the Holy
Cross 14,005

North

HOLY CROSS WILDERNESS

The Sawatch Range in central Colorado contains many lakes and the Mountain of Holy Cross, an alpine peak with snow gullies on it in the shape of a cross. At one time the mountain was a national monument; it is one of a handful of landmarks that have lost national park service protection. The mountain and the surrounding area have become one of Colorado's newest formally designated wilderness areas, although a shadow has been cast over the integrity of the area because of water diversion proposals.

Trailways has one stop per day in each direction at Minturn on its Denver-Aspen route. Westbound from Denver, the bus will only stop to let passengers off. This same route serves the Eagles Nest Wilderness further east. A White River National Forest ranger station is located in Minturn as well as several trails leading into the wilderness area.

Mount of the Holy Cross

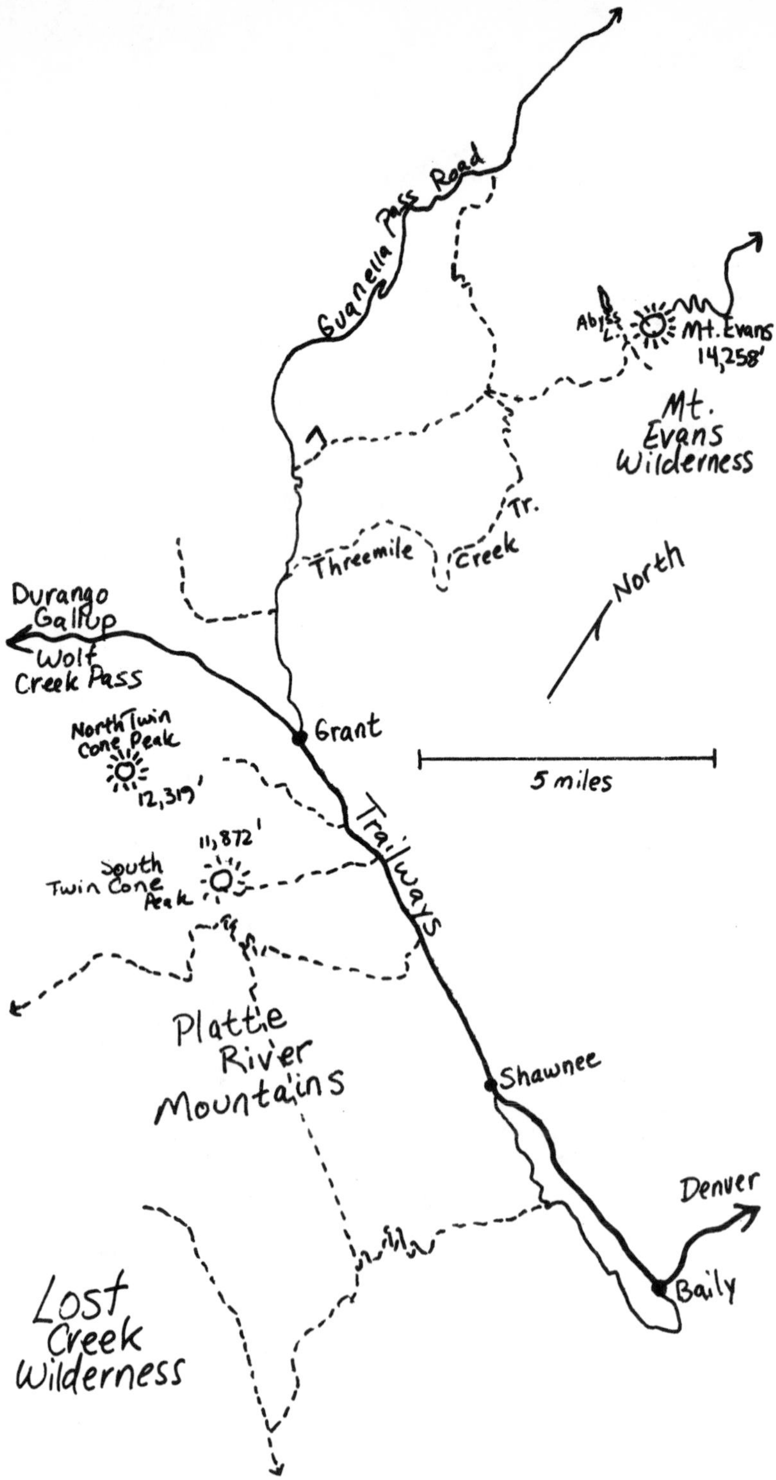
Guanella Pass Road
Abyss L.
Mt. Evans
14,258'
Mt. Evans Wilderness
Tr.
Threemile Creek
North
Durango
Gallup
Wolf Creek Pass
Grant
North Twin Cone Peak
12,319'
5 miles
Trailways
11,872'
South Twin Cone Peak
Plattie River Mountains
Shawnee
Denver
Baily
Lost Creek Wilderness

LOST CREEK WILDERNESS
MT. EVANS WILDERNESS

These two wildernesses southwest of Denver were established by congressional action late in 1980. Trailways, on its Denver—Durango—Gallup route, has one round trip daily that stops at Grant, Shawnee and Baily. (This is the same bus that will make a flag stop at the Wolf Creek Pass Trailhead of the Weminuche Wilderness.) Within three miles of Shawnee and Baily are several trails that climb into dry alpine country of the Lost Creek Wilderness high above the north fork of the South Platte River. A portion of this area has been designated as a "Further Planning Area." It is managed as wilderness, but it is not part of the area officially established as wilderness by Congress.

The most accessible trailhead within the 73,480 acre Mt. Evans Wilderness is the Threemile Creek Trail, located three miles north of Grant on Guanella Pass Road. It climbs over several ridges; one possible destination is the Abyss Lake basin nestled at the foot of 14,258 foot Mt. Evans. The summit of Mt. Evans itself is outside of its namesake wilderness because a paved road reaches the top.

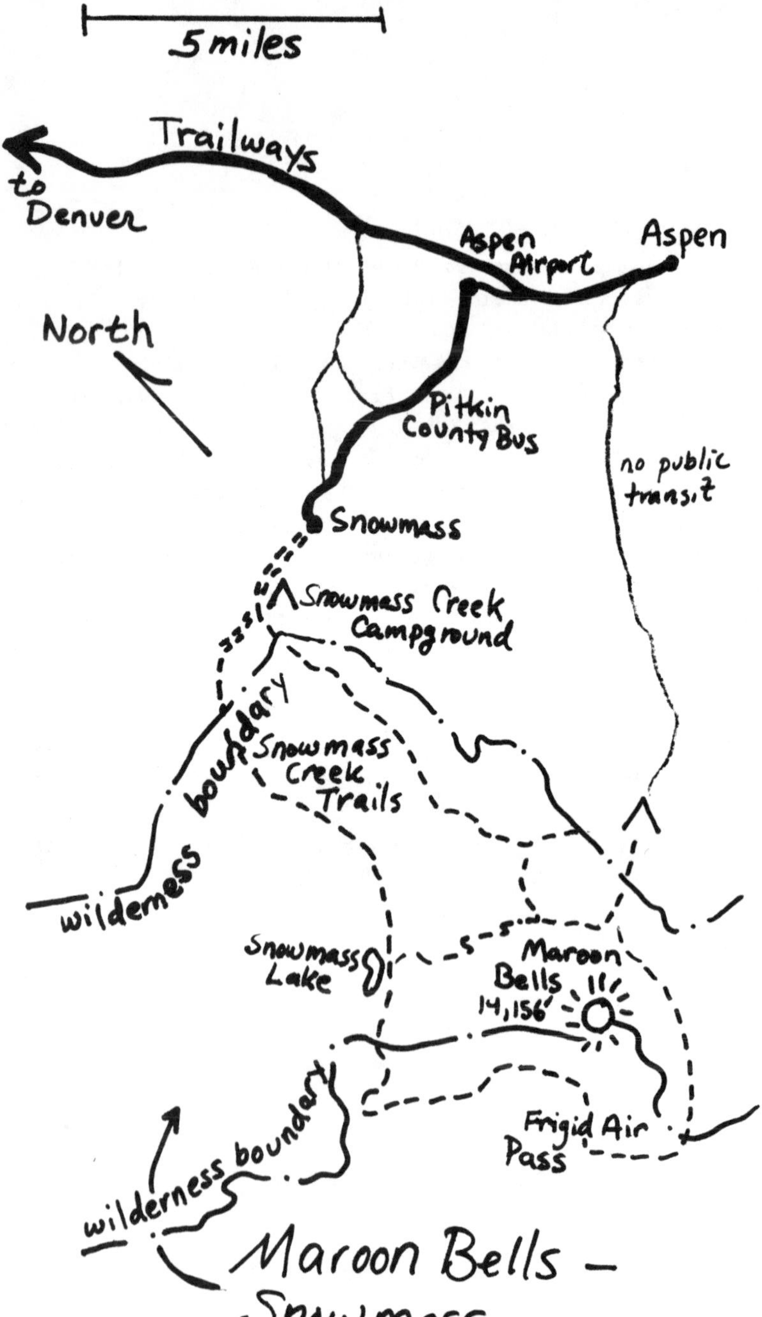

5 miles

Trailways

to Denver

Aspen Airport

Aspen

North

Pitkin County Bus

no public transit

Snowmass

Snowmass Creek Campground

wilderness boundary

Snowmass Creek Trails

Snowmass Lake

Maroon Bells 14,156'

wilderness boundary

Frigid Air Pass

Maroon Bells — Snowmass Wilderness

MAROON BELLS – SNOWMASS WILDERNESS

The Maroon Bells – Snowmass Wilderness southwest of Aspen is justly famed for alpine scenery. The 14,000 foot Maroon Bells are often featured on autumn calendars with yellowing aspens fluttering in front, the tops of the peaks just dusted with new snow. Also within this area are bear and wapiti, spruce and fir.

Trailways serves Aspen daily from Denver and Denver's Stapleton Airport. There is additional express service in the winter. Prospective winter visitors should check first with the forest service office in Aspen (806 West Hallam Street, Aspen 81611; phone: (303) 925-3445) to minimize avalanche hazards.

To get closer to the wilderness, plan to take the Pitkin County Bus, operating daily from early morning until midnight, from Aspen to Snowmass Village. From this ski area, continue west about a mile on the unpaved road leading out of the village to Snowmass Creek Campground. From here it is possible to hike south along the East Fork of Snowmass Creek. The trailhead for another route into the high country is located another half-mile past the campground and it eventually skirts Snowmass Lake, the largest body of water in the wilderness.

It is also possible to reach Aspen via commuter airline from Denver. A travel agent will be able to tell you the current carriers and fares.

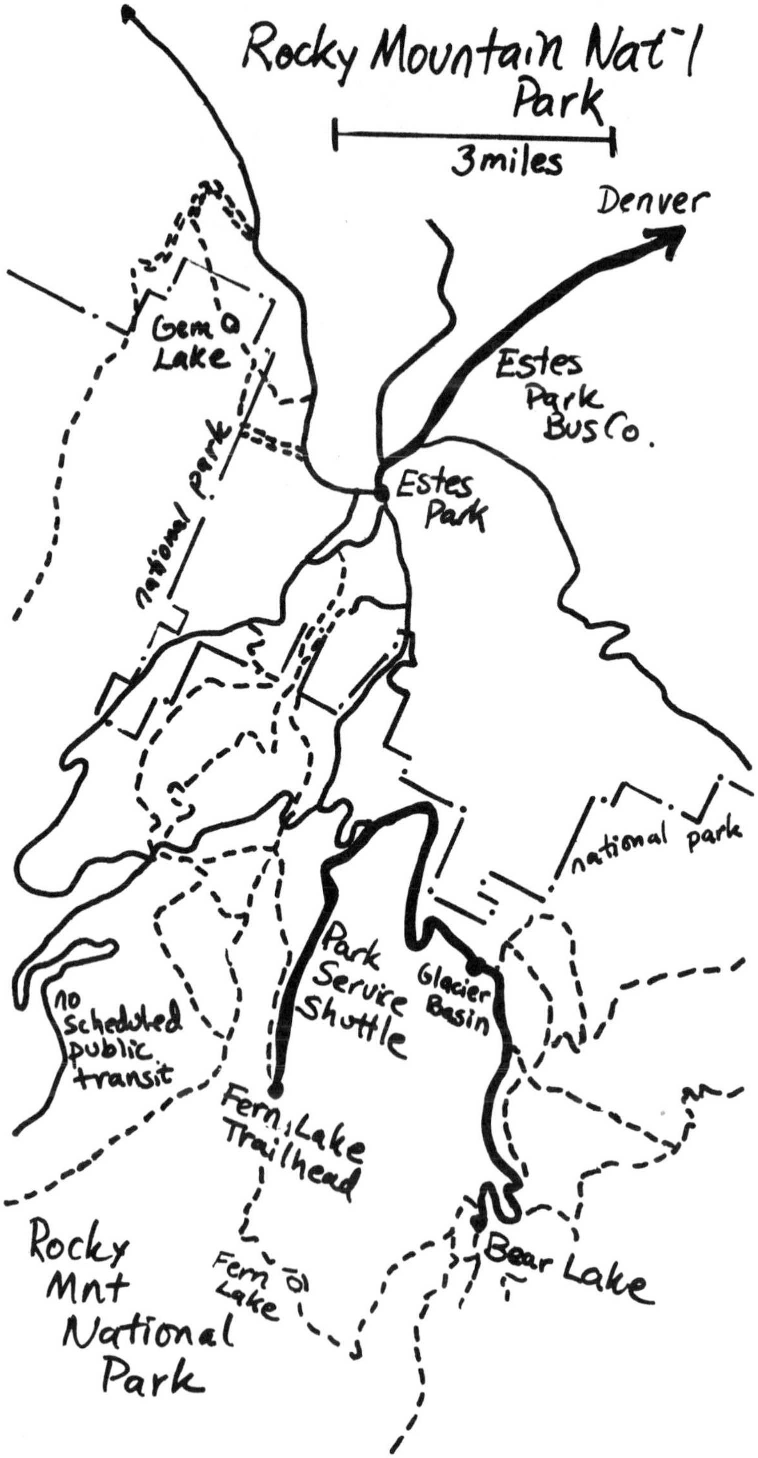

Rocky Mountain Nat'l Park

3 miles

Denver

Gem Lake

national park

Estes Park Bus Co.

Estes Park

national park

Park Service Shuttle

Glacier Basin

no scheduled public transit

Fern Lake Trailhead

Rocky Mnt National Park

Fern Lake

Bear Lake

ROCKY MOUNTAIN NATIONAL PARK

Rocky Mountain National Park protects some of the classic alpine scenery of the Colorado Rockies. Meadows, lakes, timberline terrain and three hundred miles of trail are the magnet.

Estes Park Bus Company provides year round service from Denver, Stapleton Airport and Boulder to Estes Park, which is several miles outside the park. A park information and visitor center in Estes Park can issue backcountry permits and provide additional information.

In the summer, the National Park Service operates a free shuttle bus along Bear Lake Road between Glacier Basin and Bear Lake. A less frequent bus, operating several times in the morning and afternoon, extends the route to the Fern Lake Trailhead, permitting a number of interesting loop trips. Unfortunately, at this time, the park service shuttle and the Estes Park Bus Company routes do not connect. A couple trails close to Estes Park do lead into the park, however, so it is possible to take advantage of the shuttle system.

In previous years, Estes Park Bus Company operated a bus to Meeker Park and Allenspark, at the southeast corner of the park, where there are additional trails. Contact them to see if it has been resumed. This bus company also has guided tours throughout the park area during the summer season.

Camping is permitted only in designated areas within the national park backcountry and a permit is required.

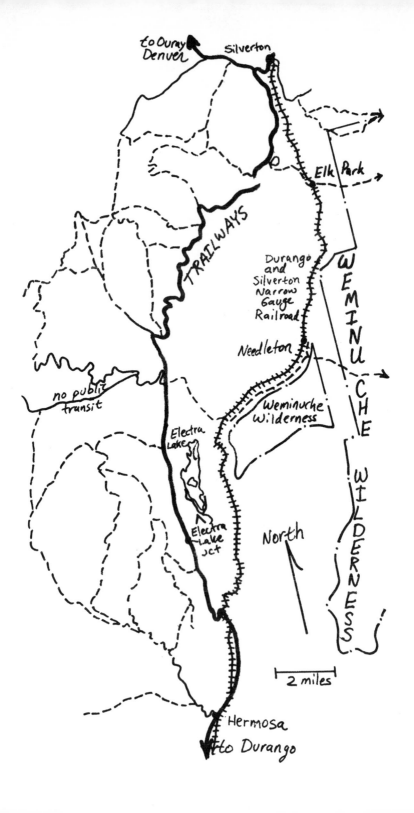

WEMINUCHE WILDERNESS

A large wilderness near the southern end of the Rocky
Mountains, high amidst the San Juan peaks, the Weminuche
Wilderness has four hundred fifty miles of trail, much
of it accessible using public transportation.

During the May to November operating season of the Durango
and Silverton Narrow Gauge Railroad from Durango to Silverton, the train makes stops at Elk Park and Needleton,
two trailheads into the wilderness to the east.

The once daily Trailways bus route from Albuquerque to
Salt Lake City (via Durango) makes flag stops at Hermosa
and Electra Lake Junction, as well as stopping in Silverton.
There are a number of hiking opportunities from each
of these stops.

Another Trailways route (not indicated on the map) travels
east from Durango twice daily to Denver and will make
a flag stop at Wolf Creek Pass. The highway crosses the
Continental Divide at this point and intersects a trail
leading south, as well as a trail which heads north into
the Weminuche Wilderness. There are several possible
destinations including small lakes and 12,000 foot peaks.

Other wilderness areas that can be reached on the two
Trailways routes mentioned include the Big Blue Wilderness
(Albuquerque to Salt Lake City) and the Lost Creek and
Mt. Evans Wildernesses (Durango to Denver). See those
descriptions for additional information.

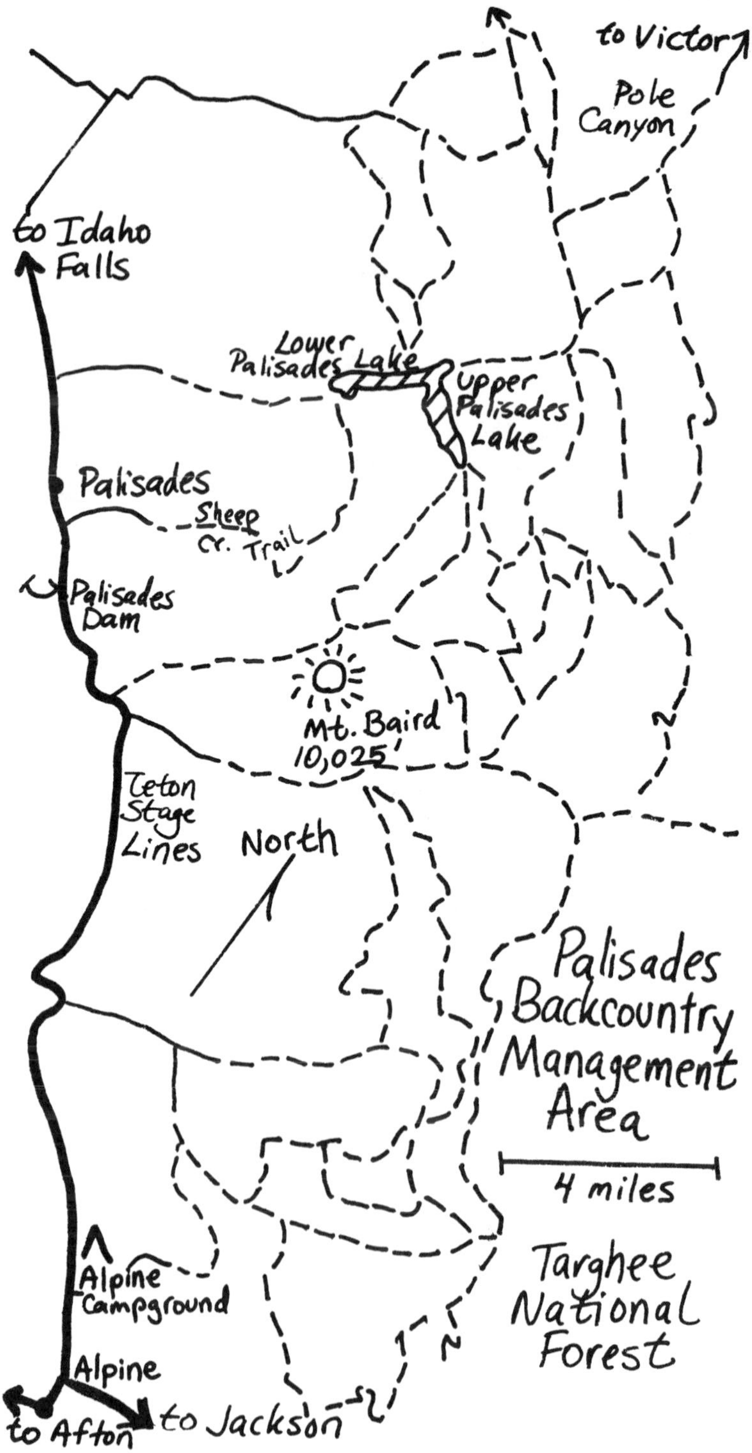

to Victor

Pole Canyon

to Idaho Falls

Lower Palisades Lake

Upper Palisades Lake

Palisades

Sheep Cr. Trail

Palisades Dam

Mt. Baird 10,025

Teton Stage Lines

North

Palisades Backcountry Management Area

4 miles

Targhee National Forest

Alpine Campground

Alpine

to Afton

to Jackson

PALISADES BACKCOUNTRY MANAGEMENT AREA

A trip to Grand Teton and Yellowstone National Parks can be combined with a visit to this scenic mountain area on the Wyoming-Idaho border. It is home to mountain goat, cutthroat trout, mule deer and 1500 wapiti.

Teton Stage Lines provides year round service, more frequent in summer, to Palisades and Victor, in Idaho, and Alpine, Wyoming, on two routes between Idaho Falls and Jackson, where there are connections to Grand Teton and Yellowstone Parks. Idaho Falls can be reached on Greyhound.

From Palisades, walk about one-half mile southeast on Highway 26 to Sheep Creek Road near the base of the Palisades Dam. Turn left and continue about two miles, through a summer home area, to reach the Sheep Creek Trail. This route climbs over a 9000 foot crest before dropping down to the 6000 foot level of the Palisades Lakes, where there is good fishing and a number of hiking alternatives. Victor is about three miles by road from a trail that travels up Pole Canyon before descending into the same drainage as Upper and Lower Palisades Lakes. From Alpine, walk northwest on Highway 26 a little over two miles to Alpine Campground. Turn right---an unmaintained trail into Long Spring Basin is located at the end of the unimproved road starting from the campground.

Much of this undesignated wilderness has been the subject of recent litigation as to whether the federal government could issue blanket leases for oil and gas exploration on public lands without considering the environmental impacts of the leasing process.

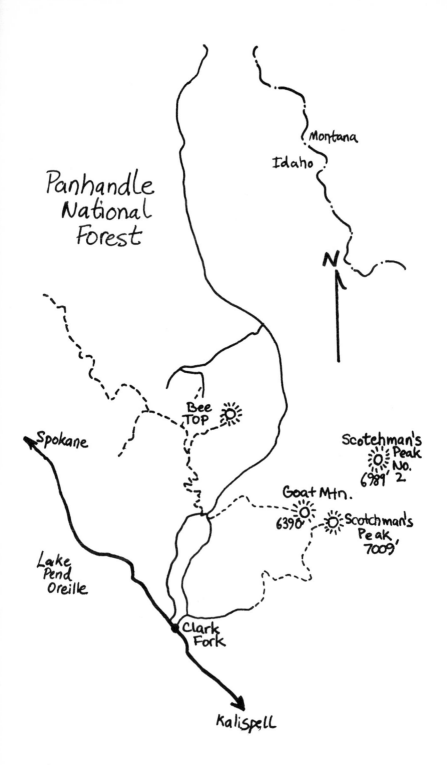

Panhandle
National
Forest

Montana

Idaho

N

Bee
TOP

Spokane

Scotchman's
Peak
No. 2
6989'

Goat Mtn.
6390'

Scotchman's
Peak
7009'

Lake
Pend
Oreille

Clark
Fork

Kalispell

PANHANDLE NATIONAL FOREST

A section of the Panhandle National Forest in northern Idaho has several short hikes available in the mountains overlooking Lake Pend Oreille. The proposed 20,000 Scotchman's Peak Wilderness is immediately to the northeast of Clark Fork, a stop on Brown Line's Kalispell to Spokane bus route. Service is available once daily in each direction except Saturdays. Intermountain Transportation and AMTRAK serve Kalispell. Spokane can be reached on Greyhound, AMTRAK and several airlines.

For the hike to the top of 7009 foot Scotchman's Peak, plan to bring all the water you will need, as there is none along the trail. Several other hiking trips are also available in this area although they are further away from Clark Fork. An extensive network of snow covered forest roads provide opportunities for crosscountry skiing and snowshoeing in winter.

Penstemon rupicola

Missoula

Lost Trail
Pass,
Sula,
Darby

8034'
Anderson
Mtn.

Montana
Idaho

North

Anderson
Creek
Tr.

West
Bigholes

Lost
Trail
Stage

Gibbonsville

Stein Mtn.
8555

Salmon
River Cyn.

North
Fork

Salmon

WEST BIGHOLES

On the Montana—Idaho border and the Continental Divide, this area has been proposed as a 51,000 acre wilderness. It includes forested ridges and views down the nearby main fork of the Salmon River. In September, 1805, Lewis and Clark struggled over nearby Lost Trail Pass and this area remains relatively unsettled to this day.

Lost Trail Stage provides service from Salmon to Darby, Montana six days weekly. Three days weekly service is extended north to the Missoula Greyhound station and by arrangement to the Missoula Airport. The stop at Gibbonsville is close to a trail up Anderson Creek reaching the top of Anderson Mountain. Two and a half miles south of Sula, at the Sula Ranger Station, a trail heads east towards the Continental Divide. The bus stop at North Fork is also close to several trails; a couple of loop trips are possible.

It is possible to reach Salmon using Salmon River Stages from Pocatello and Idaho Falls. Pocatello and Idaho Falls are both Greyhound stops and AMTRAK serves Pocatello. Missoula has both Greyhound and major airline connections.

Cabinet Mountains
Wilderness

N

to Spokane
Seattle

Brown Lines

AMTRAK

Libby

to Kalispell
Chicago

Parameter Creek Trail

7345

Wilderness

Boundary

Cabinet
Mountains
Wilderness

2 miles

CABINET MOUNTAINS WILDERNESS

In the northwest corner of Montana, this wilderness has more of the flavor of the thicker, wetter forests of Oregon and Washington than most other areas in Montana. Several peaks breach 8000 feet elevation.

Brown Lines, on its Kalispell to Spokane route, stops in Libby daily except Saturdays. AMTRAK's Empire Builder from Seattle to Chicago also stops in Libby daily. A trail two and a half miles out of town enters the wilderness via Parameter Creek. More information can be obtained at the Kootenai National Forest headquarters in Libby.

Cornus canadenis

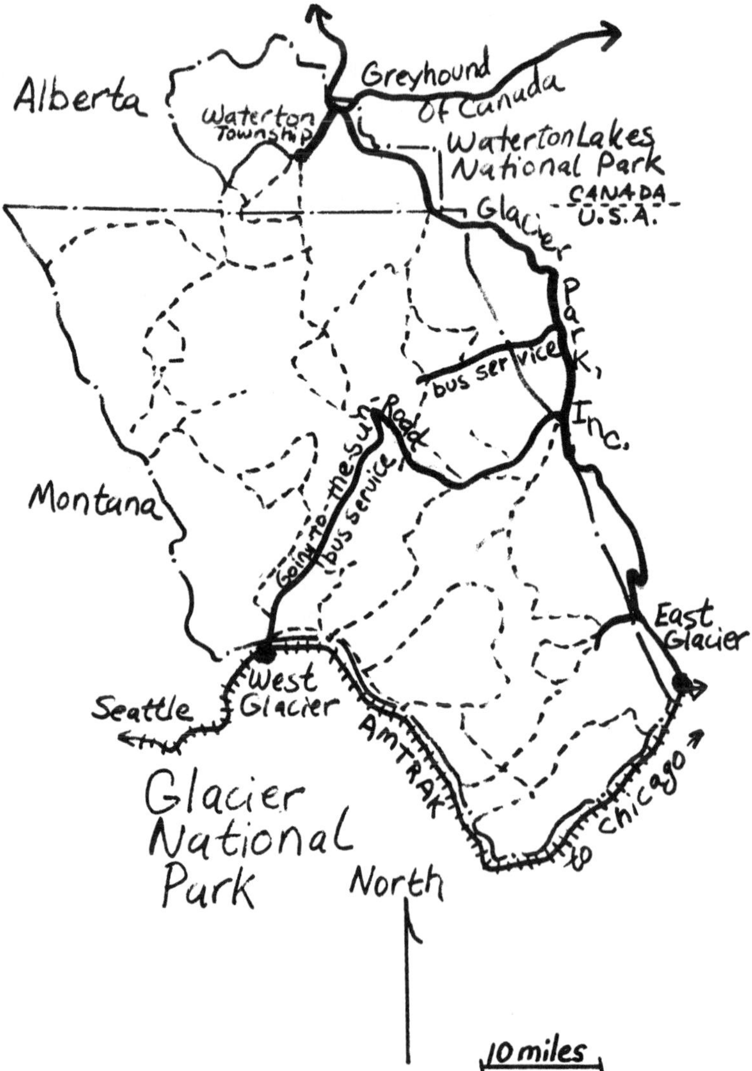
Alberta
Waterton Township
Greyhound of Canada
Waterton Lakes National Park
CANADA
U.S.A.
Glacier Park, Inc.
bus service
Going-to-the-Sun Road
bus service
Montana
East Glacier
West Glacier
Seattle
AMTRAK
to Chicago
Glacier National Park
North
10 miles

GLACIER NATIONAL PARK

Glacier National Park is one of the finest parks in North America, not only for seven hundred miles of trail, precipitious peaks and flower carpeted meadows, but also for its accessibility to public transportation users.

AMTRAK stops in East Glacier and West Glacier daily year round on its Chicago-Seattle Empire Builder route. Both train stations are just outside the park boundary, but within walking distance of several long distance backpacking trailheads. Permits are required for overnight camping at designated backcountry campsites and can be obtained, providing space is available, from the information center at West Glacier or the ranger station at East Glacier.

In addition, Glacier Park, Inc., the park concessionaire, has summer bus service over most of park's roads including the scenic Going-to-the-Sun Road. The designated routes include bus service from Glacier Park Lodge in East Glacier to the Prince of Wales Hotel in Waterton National Park to the north. Glacier Park, Inc. is flexible about letting hikers on and off buses at trailheads along their routes; call them beforehand to request and reserve such stopovers.

Finally, in the past several small bus companies have provided bus service to Glacier Park from nearby cities in Montana, although AMTRAK remains the most consistent means of reaching the park. Contact the National Park Service in Glacier for updated information on this public transportation possibility.

See the Waterton Lakes National Park description under Alberta for information on reaching Waterton (and by connection, Glacier) from Canada.

☀ Gallatin Peak 11,012'

North

Spanish Peaks Wilderness

North Fork Trail

wilderness boundary

Big Sky

to Bozeman

TWA Services

2 miles

to West Yellowstone

SPANISH PEAKS WILDERNESS

This is a scenic, high altitude wilderness with peaks up to 11,000 feet elevation and it often bypassed by recreation seekers headed for nearby Yellowstone.

During the summer, TWA Services operates a bus daily from Bozeman and the Bozeman Airport to Yellowstone Park. Enroute, one stop is made at the Big Sky resort and ski area.

From Big Sky Meadow Village, walk northwest on the Middle Fork Road leading to the ski area and turn right onto the unimproved road adjacent to an old sawmill. This road runs parallel to the North Fork of the Gallatin River and provides access to the North Fork Trail. The wilderness boundary and Summit Lake are reached after a tough nine mile hike from the trailhead. One consolation is that this particular trail is lightly used.

During fall, winter and spring, bus service to Big Sky is once weekly.

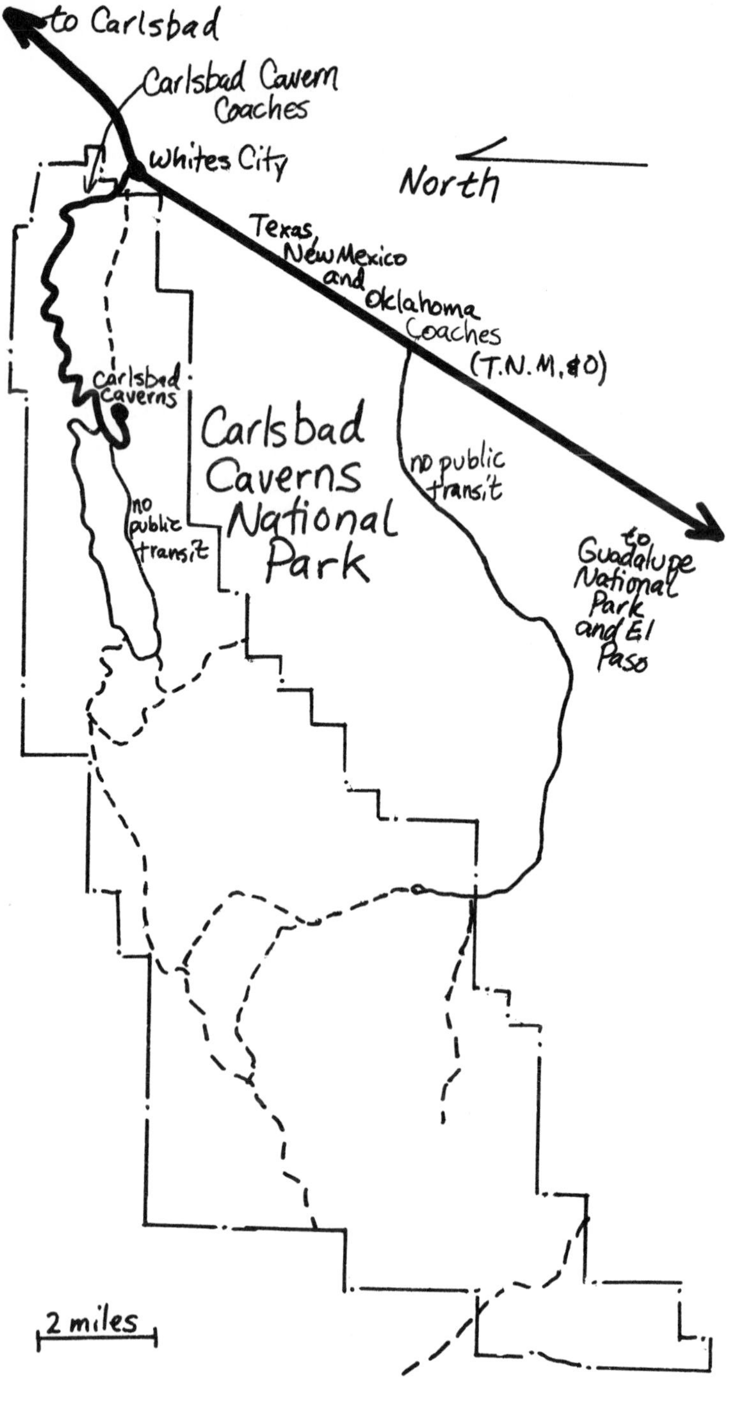

to Carlsbad

Carlsbad Cavern
Coaches

Whites City

North

Texas,
New Mexico
and
Oklahoma
Coaches
(T.N.M.&O)

Carlsbad
Caverns

no public
transit

Carlsbad
Caverns
National
Park

no public
transit

to
Guadalupe
National
Park
and El
Paso

2 miles

CARLSBAD CAVERNS NATIONAL PARK

The massive underground grottos of the park are the main attraction. For visitors who wish to linger and appreciate the rugged desert and mountain terrain, thirty five miles of trail are available. Plan to carry all of the water you will need; a required backcountry permit, topographic maps and information on the lightly used trail system can be obtained at the park visitor center. Wood fires are prohibited and campsites must be at least $\frac{1}{4}$ mile away from and out of view of any road.

T.N.M. & O. Coaches serve the park entrance once daily from both Carlsbad and El Paso. The bus service from the park entrance to the cavern and visitor center is provided by Carlsbad Cavern Coaches. The bus schedule is arranged so that a one day tour of the cavern is possible. One can then continue on or return to Carlsbad or El Paso.

The T.N.M. & O. bus route to El Paso passes through Guadalupe Mountains National Park, a good hiking area, but unfortunately there are no scheduled stops near the park.

El Paso and Carlsbad can both be reached on Trailways or Greyhound affiliated carriers.

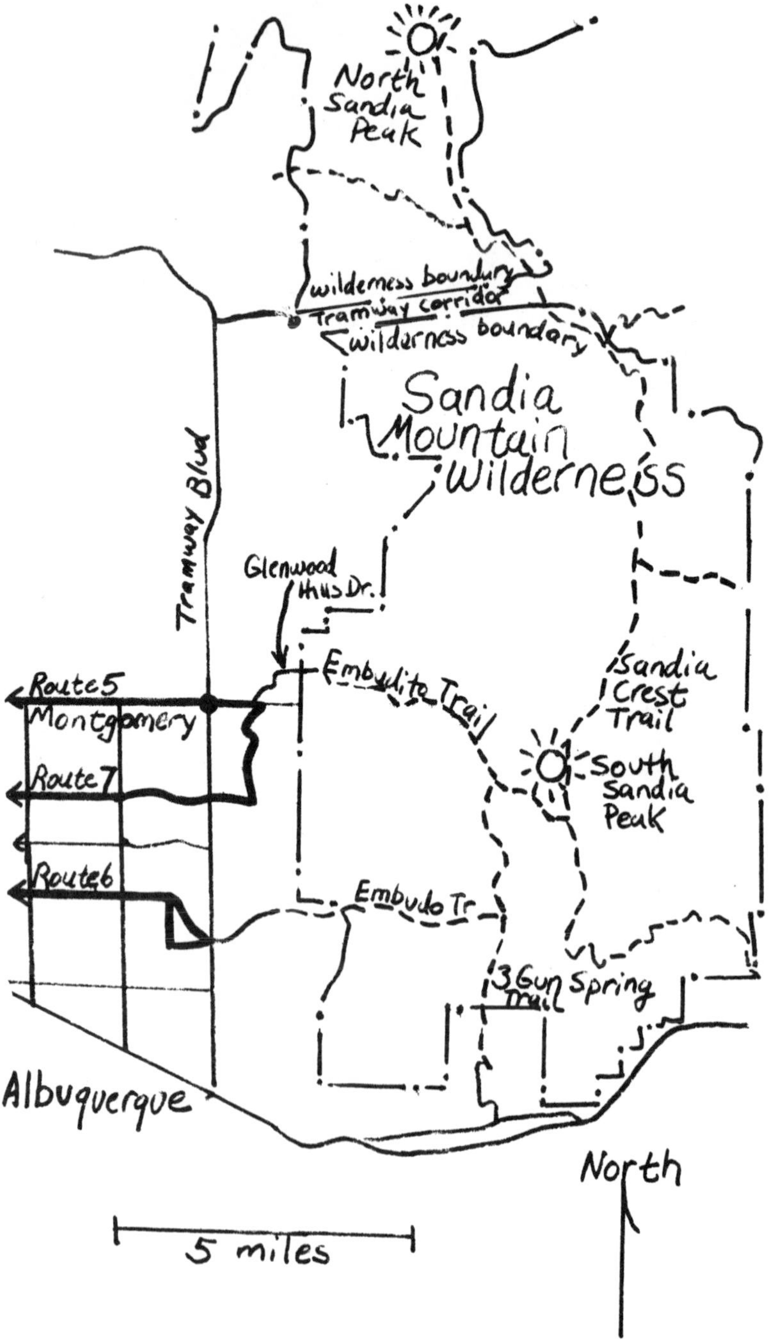

North Sandia Peak

wilderness boundary
Tramway corridor
wilderness boundary

Sandia Mountain Wilderness

Tramway Blvd

Glenwood Hills Dr.

Route 5
Montgomery

Route 7

Route 6

Embudito Trail

Sandia Crest Trail

South Sandia Peak

Embudo Tr.

3 Gun Spring Trail

Albuquerque

North

5 miles

SANDIA MOUNTAIN WILDERNESS

Close to Albuquerque, the Sandia Mountains rise abruptly out of the New Mexico landscape. Two trails in particular are good for bus users, starting out of the base of the mountains in the Albuquerque suburbs.

To get to the Embudito Trail, take Albuquerque Sun Tran Route 5 to the end of the line or Route 7 to the corner of Glenwood Hills Drive and Montgomery (peak hour service only). Route 7 operates weekdays only while Route 5 provides service on Saturdays also. The trail begins at the end of Glenwood Hills Drive and climbs 3200 feet in five and a half miles to the Sandia Crest Trail, itself a twenty-seven mile backpack. Water and a shelter are available at Oso Spring before reaching the Crest Trail.

A less well defined route is the Embudo Trail, starting from the flood control dam at the end of Indian School Road. Route 6 of Albuquerque Sun Tran operates six days weekly, except holidays along Indian School Road; the turnaround bus stop at Constitution Avenue and Indian School Road is about three miles west of the trailhead. The trail climbs 3200 feet in elevation up Embudo Canyon before joining the Three Gun Spring Trail, a route connecting with the Embudito and Sandia Crest Trails.

Cibola National Forest headquarters in Albuquerque is served by Sun Tran Route 7 and Route 50 serves the airport (six days weekly, daylight hours). Routes 7 and 50 can both be boarded in downtown Albuquerque at the corner of 5th Street and Gold Avenue, about five blocks from AMTRAK, Greyhound and Trailways. Route 5 stops at Girard Blvd. and Central Avenue near the University of New Mexico campus. Connections can be made with this route and the downtown transportation terminals via Routes 1, 2, 3 and 12 which travel down Central Avenue from the downtown area.

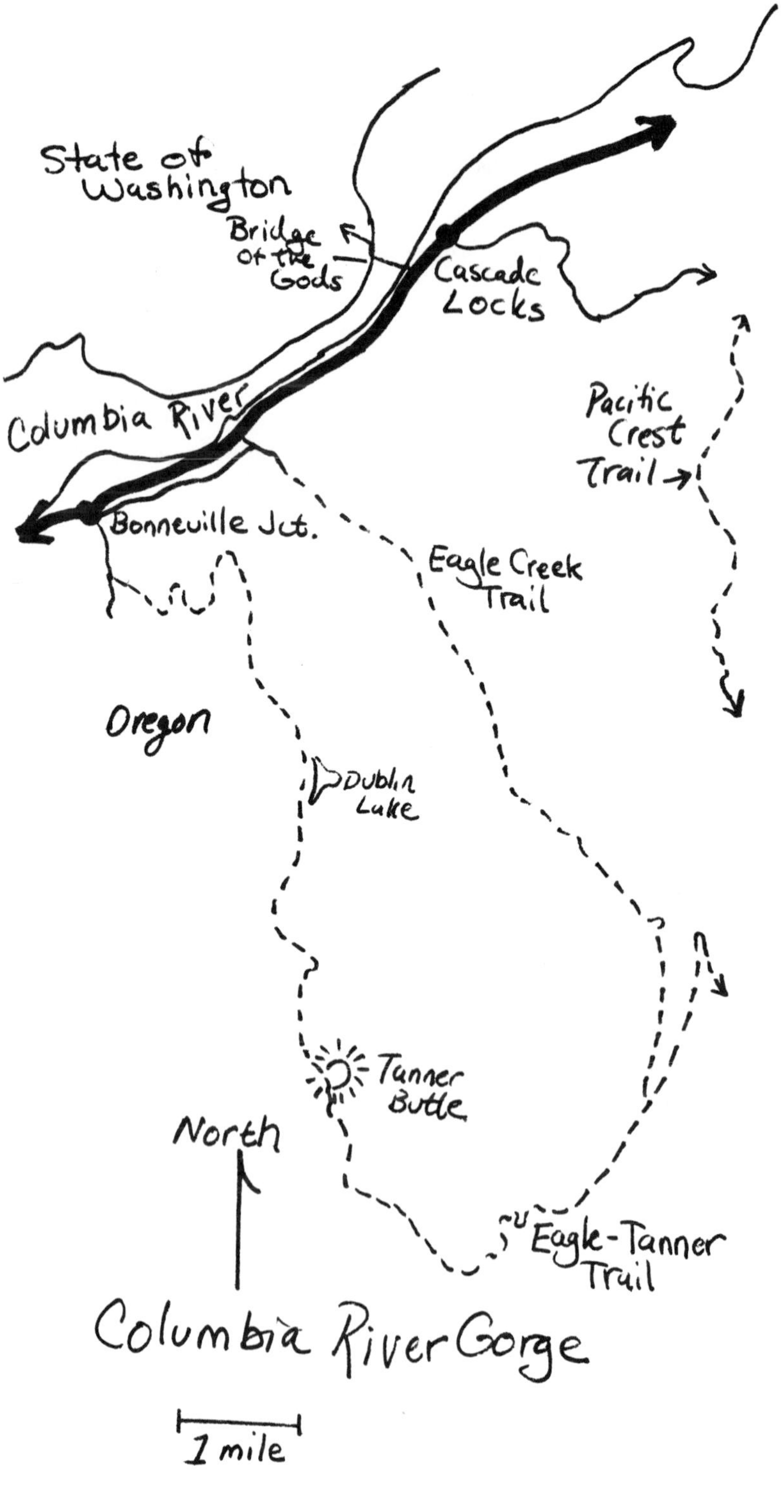

State of
Washington

Bridge
of the
Gods

Cascade
Locks

Columbia River

Pacific
Crest
Trail →

Bonneville Jct.

Eagle Creek
Trail

Oregon

Dublin
Lake

Tanner
Butte

North

Eagle-Tanner
Trail

Columbia River Gorge

1 mile

COLUMBIA RIVER GORGE

The Columbia River's Gorge, cut through the Cascades, has left a vertical wilderness extending from the low elevation of the river to the highest mountain in Oregon. (See the Mt. Hood Wilderness description for other public transportation in this area.) Hiking opportunities are particularly good within this area close to metropolitan Portland.

Bonneville Junction, which is served once daily from Portland by Greyhound (as a highway flag stop) is about two miles from the trailhead to Dublin Lake and Tanner Butte. The Eagle Creek Trailhead is located about three miles east of Bonneville Jct. From here it is 13.2 miles to the Pacific Crest Trail and 7.6 miles to the Eagle-Tanner Trail. The Eagle-Tanner Trail is a five mile long trail intersecting the Tanner Butte Trail 7.8 miles south of its trailhead, thus allowing a nice three day loop trip, with a return to Bonneville Jct.

Greyhound also provides direct access to the Pacific Crest Trail, having several flag stops daily at Cascade Locks, where the Crest Trail enters Washington.

Both Eagle and Tanner Creek Valleys contain exposed rock called the Eagle Creek Formation, which contains petrified wood and leaf fossils.

The future of the Columbia River Gorge has been the subject of a long-standing land management dispute. Wilderness designation has been proposed for 52,000 roadless acres centering on Eagle Creek.

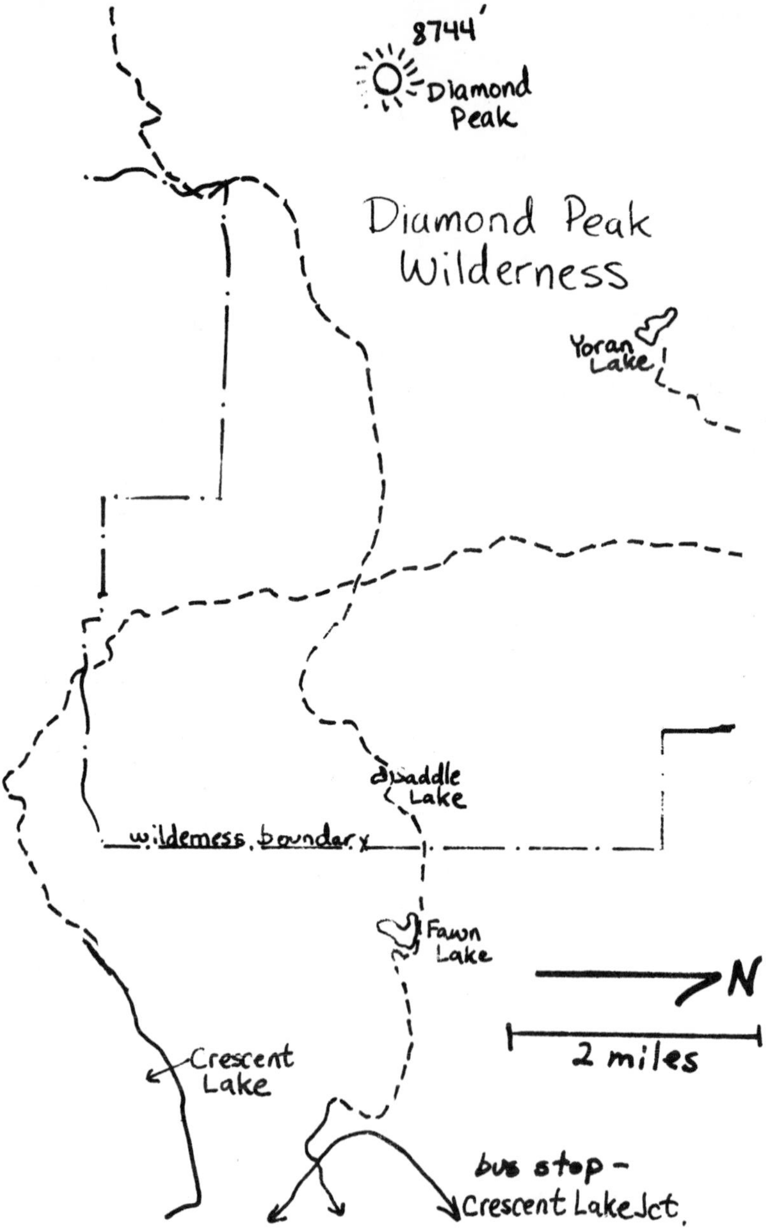

8744'
Diamond
Peak

Diamond Peak
Wilderness

Yoran
Lake

Saddle
Lake

wilderness boundary

Fawn
Lake

N

2 miles

Crescent
Lake

bus stop -
Crescent Lake Jct.

DIAMOND PEAK WILDERNESS

A relatively small area, the Diamond Peak Wilderness spreads over the Cascade Crest in southern Oregon and has about fifty miles of trail. Diamond Peak is an old Cascade volcano rising above a lake dotted sloping plateau country that is accessible to public transportation users. The predominate tree cover is lodgepole pine and these eastern slopes of the Cascades are sunnier and dryer than the wet maritime forest on the west side.

Greyhound has three round trips daily between Klamath Falls and Eugene that make stops at Crescent Lake Junction. Two and a half miles up Crescent Lake Road, the Fawn Lake trail climbs into the wilderness. This eastern portion of the wilderness is administered by the Deschutes National Forest. Klamath Falls and Eugene are both on AMTRAK's Coast Starlight route and can also be reached on both Greyhound and Trailways.

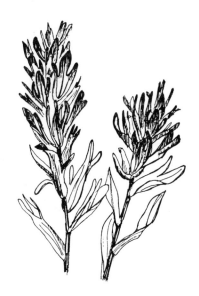

Castilleja miniata

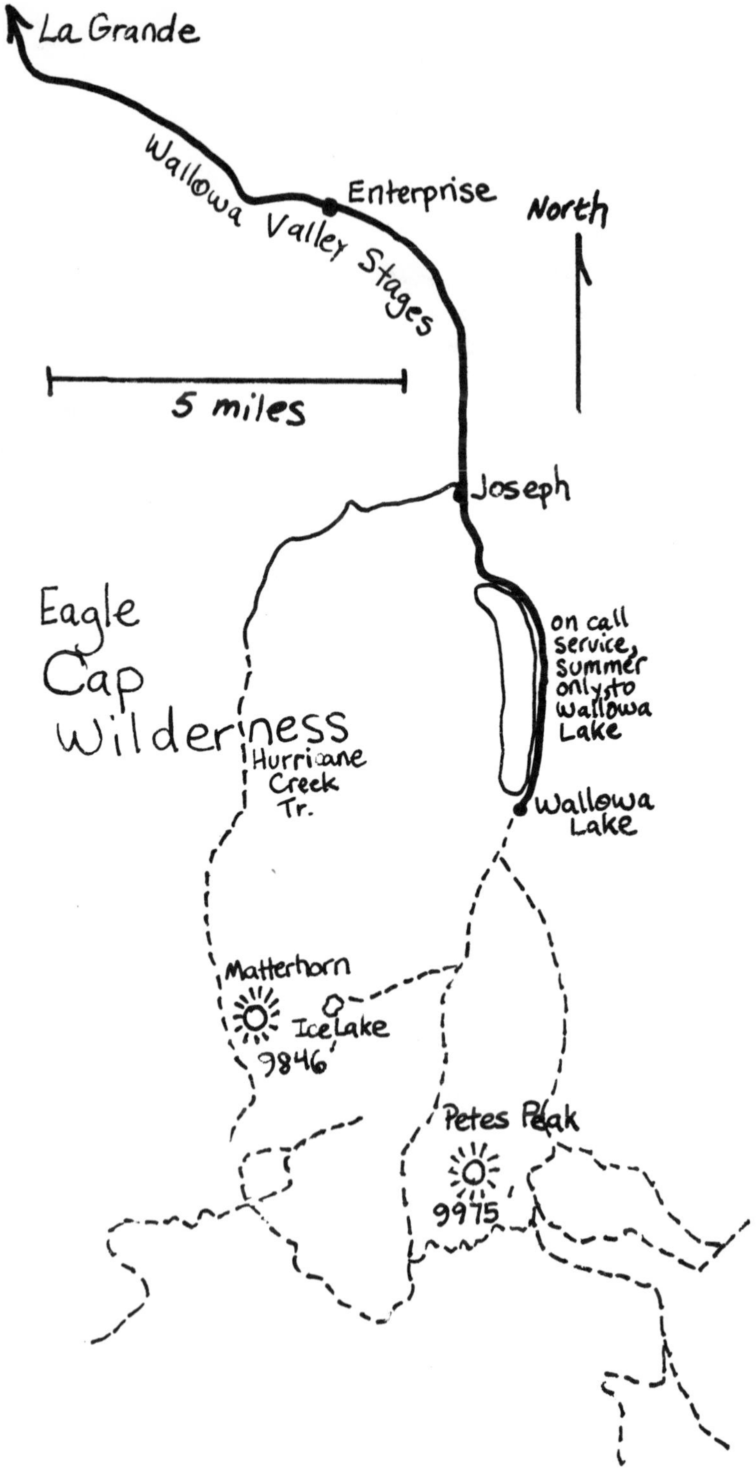
La Grande
Wallowa Valley Stages
Enterprise
North
5 miles
Joseph
Eagle Cap Wilderness
on call service, summer only to Wallowa Lake
Hurricane Creek Tr.
Wallowa Lake
Matterhorn
Ice Lake
9846
Petes Peak
9975

EAGLE CAP WILDERNESS

The Wallowa Mountains in northeastern Oregon were originally the home of the Nez Perce tribe and the Indian leader Thunder-Traveling-to-Loftier-Mountain-Heights, who became better known as Chief Joseph. The Eagle Cap Wilderness protects much of these beautiful mountains, making it one of the finest hiking areas in the Pacific Northwest.

Wallowa Valley Stages provides service once daily except Sundays and holidays from the La Grande Greyhound station to Joseph. In summer only, on call service is available to Wallowa Lake, an Oregon state park that is the trailhead for a network of routes leading into the center of the wilderness. Service the rest of the year is to within six miles of Wallowa Lake. Greyhound reaches La Grande three times daily in each direction on its Portland to Boise route. AMTRAK's Pioneer, which serves Salt Lake City, Boise, Portland and Seattle daily, also stops in La Grande.

Erythronium grandiflorum

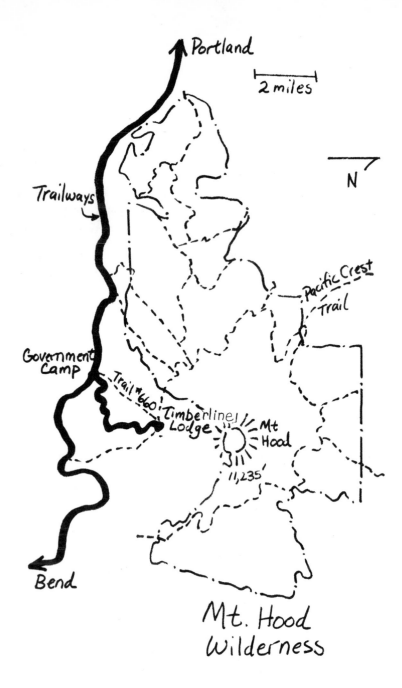

Portland

2 miles

N

Trailways

Pacific Crest
Trail

Government
Camp

Trail #660
Timberline
Lodge

Mt
Hood

11,235'

Bend

Mt. Hood
Wilderness

MT. HOOD WILDERNESS

Close to Portland, with 11,235 foot Mt. Hood dominating the skyline, this wilderness is popular in summer for backpacking and in winter for snowshoeing and ski touring.

Trailways provides service to Government Camp three times daily in each direction on its Portland – Bend route. From Government Camp, it is possible to hike Trail #660 to Timberline Lodge. From the Lodge, hiking is available north or south on the Pacific Crest Trail. It is also to reach the Lodge from Government Camp using the Timberline Lodge• Shuttle, operating a number of times daily. The shuttle frequency varies seasonally.

A good extended backpack would be a hike north on the Pacific Crest Trail to the Columbia River. Greyhound provides public transportation to Cascade Locks, where the Crest Trail crosses into Washington. See the Columbia Gorge description for more information.

Mt. Hood

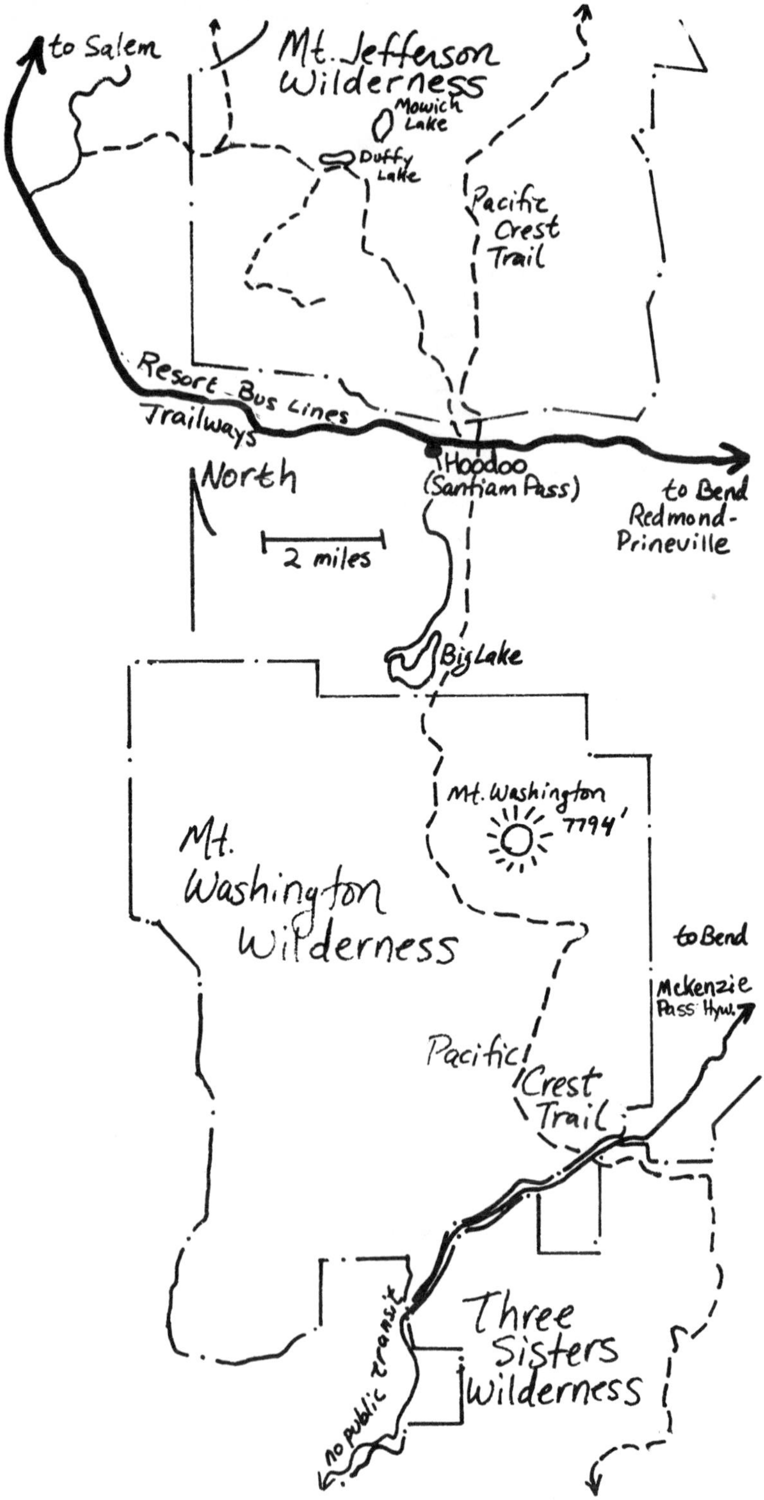

to Salem

Mt. Jefferson
Wilderness

Mowich
Lake

Duffy
Lake

Pacific
Crest
Trail

Resort Bus Lines
Trailways

North

2 miles

Hoodoo
(Santiam Pass)

to Bend
Redmond-
Prineville

Big Lake

Mt. Washington 7794'

Mt.
Washington
Wilderness

to Bend

McKenzie
Pass Hwy.

Pacific
Crest
Trail

no public transit

Three
Sisters
Wilderness

MT. JEFFERSON WILDERNESS
MT. WASHINGTON WILDERNESS

These two wildernesses, separated by only the Santiam
Pass Highway, present two differing images of the Cascades.
Alpine lakes, thick forests and glacially derived scenery
are the hallmarks of the Mt. Jefferson Wilderness, while
the Mt. Washington Wilderness exhibits less subtly the
forces of volcanic upheaval that created the Cascades.

Resort Bus Line, on its daily route from the Portland
International Airport to Bend, has a stop at Hoodoo, adjacent
to the Pacific Crest Trail crossing of the highway. Walking
north on the trail, one enters the Mt. Jefferson Wilderness,
walking south, the Mt. Washington Wilderness. In addition
to the Portland Airport stop, Resort Bus Line also has
intermediate stops in Portland at AMTRAK and at Trailways
and Greyhound in Salem before reaching Hoodoo. A hike
through the Mt. Washington Wilderness on the Pacific Crest
Trail eventually crosses the McKenzie Pass Highway, entering
the Three Sisters Wilderness, with its hundreds of lakes
and two hundred and forty mile trail system.

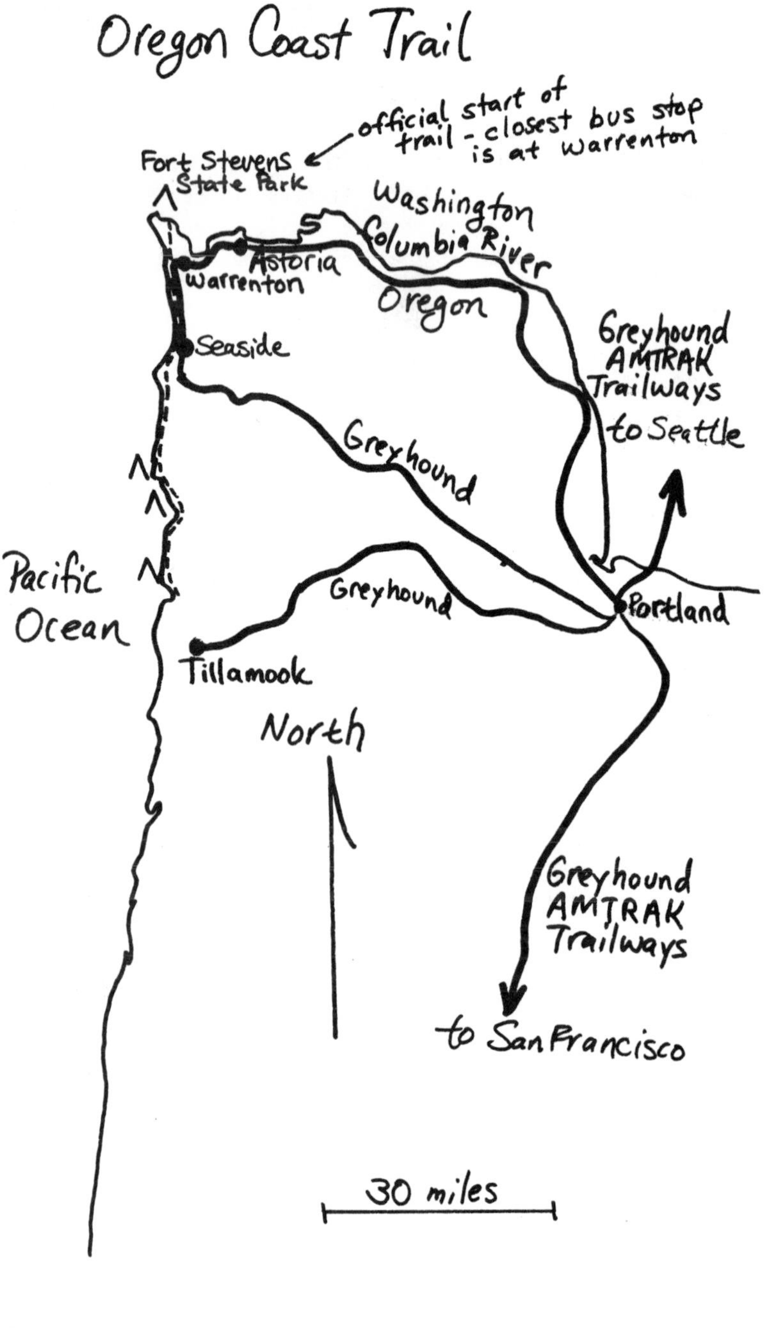

Oregon Coast Trail

official start of
trail - closest bus stop
is at Warrenton

Fort Stevens
State Park

Washington
Columbia River

Oregon

Astoria

Warrenton

Seaside

Greyhound
AMTRAK
Trailways

to Seattle

Greyhound

Pacific
Ocean

Greyhound

Portland

Tillamook

North

Greyhound
AMTRAK
Trailways

to San Francisco

30 miles

OREGON COAST TRAIL

Eventually the completed Oregon Coast Trail will permit hiking the entire Oregon coastline. The sixty-four miles between the Columbia River and Tillamook Bay make up the largest existing section. Several campgrounds are available along the route.

Greyhound provides service from Portland along Highway 101, parallel to the trail: to Astoria at the north end, to Seaside in the middle and to Tillamook. Service is several times daily for each of these routes and varies seasonally.

The Oregon State Parks and Recreation Branch (address in Appendix II) has a free brochure describing the trail, as well as an inexpensive guidebook.

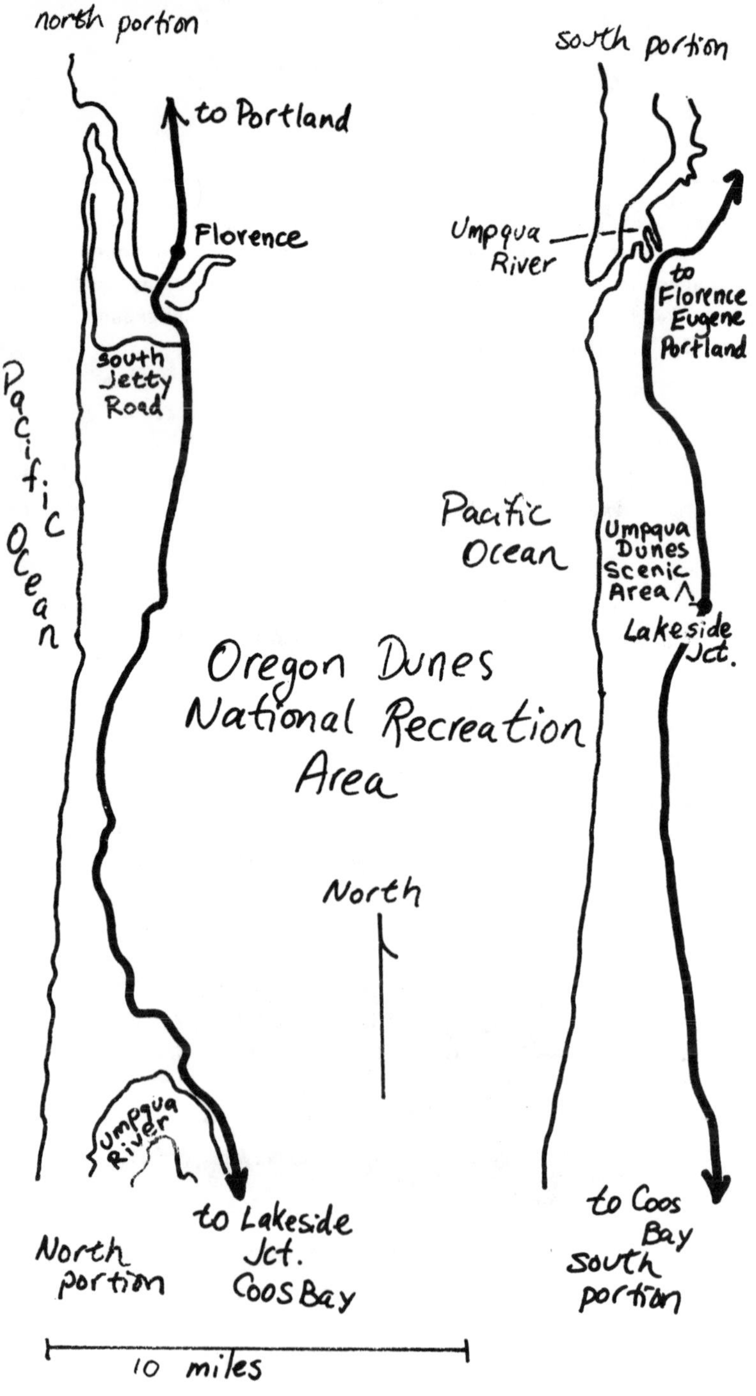

north portion

to Portland

Florence

south Jetty Road

Pacific Ocean

south portion

Umpqua River

to Florence Eugene Portland

Pacific Ocean

Umpqua Dunes Scenic Area ∧

Lakeside Jct.

Oregon Dunes National Recreation Area

North

Umpqua River

to Lakeside Jct. Coos Bay

North portion

to Coos Bay

south portion

10 miles

OREGON DUNES NATIONAL RECREATION AREA

The Oregon Dunes National Recreation Area contains a
diverse series of biological communities along forty
miles of southwest Oregon shoreline, including exposed
coast, salt marshes, dunes, transition areas and maritime
forest. Much of the area is open to off-road vehicle
use, but the Umpqua Dunes Scenic Area is not and it is
located a short distance from Lakeside Junction, served
by Greyhound four times daily from Coos Bay and Portland.
Adjacent to the highway are North and Middle Eel Campgrounds. Trails from both camping areas lead a short
distance out into the sand dunes. The beach is about
two miles distant after a walk through some of the most
impressive sand dunes in North America. Backcountry camping
is permitted within the scenic area, but plan to bring
water with you.

One other backcountry area is available by walking south
from Florence, another Greyhound stop, about three miles
to the South Jetty Road. Walking west into the recreation
area, the sand dunes, salt marsh and tidal flats to the
north of the road are closed to vehicle use and present
additional hiking opportunities.

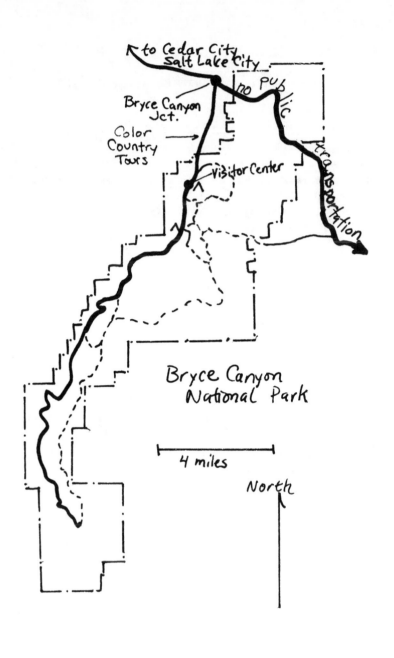

to Cedar City
Salt Lake City

no public

transportation

Bryce Canyon
Jct.

Color
Country
Tours

Visitor Center

Bryce Canyon
National Park

4 miles

North

BRYCE CANYON NATIONAL PARK

Bryce Canyon embraces some of the scenic plateau country of southeastern Utah and because of its relatively high altitude, it is one of the few southwestern parks that is comfortable to hike during the summer.

Color Country Tours provides transportation to Bryce from May to October three times weekly from Cedar City. The bus service is primarily designed as a one day tour of the park with stops at Zion Canyon Overlook, Cedar Breaks National Monument and Navajo Lake before reaching the park visitor center. One way transportation is possible for people wanting to use the park's hiking trail system. Cedar City can be reached using Greyhound and Trailways, as well as Sky West Aviation, which flies in from Salt Lake City.

downtown
Salt Lake City

2 miles

North

Utah
Transit
Authority
Route 21

3100
E

Dimple
Dell Rd.

Bell
Canyon
Trail

Little
Cottonwood
Canyon
Road

winter
ski bus
only

Lone
Peak,
11,253'

Lake
Hardy

Lone
Peak
Wilderness

Alpine
(not served
by public
transit)

no public
transit

WASATCH RANGE — LONE PEAK WILDERNESS

The Lone Peak Wilderness was Utah's first congressionally designated wilderness area and the protection of this 30,000 acre roadless tract so close to Salt Lake City was a major environmental victory. Wilderness protection in Utah has lagged behind almost all other western states largely due to an unfavorable political climate. The view from the top of 11,253 foot Lone Peak of the sprawling Salt Lake Valley metropolitan area should serve as reminder enough of how little wilderness we have left.

From the corner of Little Cottonwood Canyon Road and 3100 East, the turnaround point of Utah Transit Authority Route 21 (service four times daily, except Sundays and holidays), walk south on 3100 E. about one-half mile where the road makes a sharp right angle turn. Immediately after this, turn left onto Dimple Dell Road and continue one-quarter mile to Bell Canyon Road, turn left, continue another one-quarter mile to Wasatch Blvd., turn left again and you will be at the Bell Canyon Trail into the Lone Peak Wilderness.

In many places in the upper canyon, the trail has been obscured by avalanche and rockslide debris. At the end of the canyon, after a climb of 5000 feet in seven miles, a saddle provides access over the ridge to Lake Hardy. Near this lake are a number of good campsites and routes to the tops of several nearby peaks, including Lone Peak, the highest.

Get on the Route 21 bus along 4th South Street in downtown Salt Lake City. This is about five blocks from AMTRAK and the Greyhound and Trailways depots. Utah Transit Authority Route 50 serves the Airport.

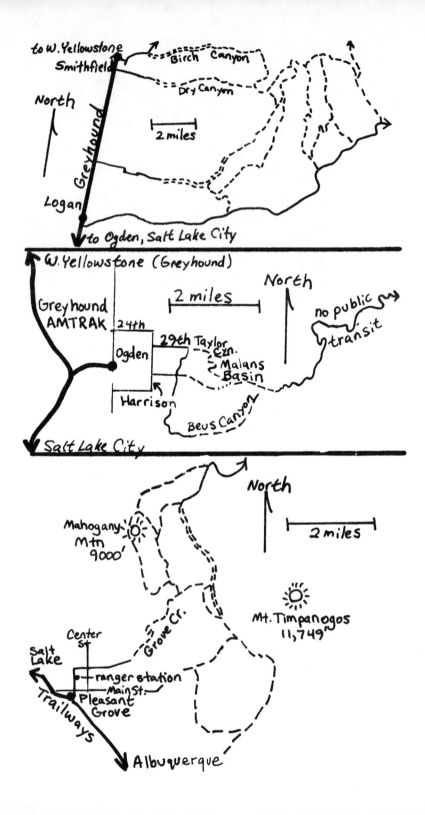

WASATCH RANGE - OTHER ACCESS

Rising behind the population center of Utah, the Wasatch Range offers a number of ski-touring and hiking choices.

The Utah Transit Authority (UTA) has a winter ski bus system that serves resorts at Alta, Brighton, Snowbird and Solitude. Buses can be boarded at a variety of locations including the Salt Lake City International Airport and along West Temple Street in downtown Salt Lake City. All four resorts are in the Wasatch National Forest. Discuss possible routes from these ski areas beforehand with people at the national forest headquarters in Salt Lake City to avoid avalanches and other winter hazards.

In other seasons, several hiking trips can be started from transit terminals or stops. A loop trip up Waterfall Canyon through Malans Basin and down Taylor Canyon can be initiated from the end of Buchanan Avenue, near 29th Street, in Ogden. This trail is less than three miles from the AMTRAK station and Greyhound and Trailways depots. Local bus service, provided by UTA, Northern Division, can get you even closer.

Pleasant Grove, south of Salt Lake City, is served by Trailways once daily on its Salt Lake-Albuquerque route and it is within three miles of routes into the Mt. Timpanogos Scenic Area.

A hike up Birch Canyon into high country near Mt. Naomi can be started at the Smithfield Greyhound station, which is served several times daily on the Salt Lake-West Yellowstone route. From Smithfield, walk east on 100 North. After two blocks and a short turn to the right, turn left onto Canyon Road. Follow this road about a mile to Birch Canyon Road. Turn right; the road deteriorates into a trail up the stream-watered canyon in about a mile and a half.

Zion National Park

Virgin River

West Rim Trail

Cedar City

Zion Lodge

Visitor Center

Color Country Tours

5 miles

North

ZION NATIONAL PARK

Zion's steep walled canyons and vaulted rock formations are an attractive magnet for hikers, particularly in the cooler months of spring and fall.

Color Country Tours provides transportation to Zion from Cedar City three times weekly from May to October. Like a similar bus route to Bryce Canyon, the service to the park is primarily designed for people on a one day tour, but one way and overnight hikers will be accomodated. Cedar City can be reached using Greyhound and Trailways and also Sky West Aviation from Salt Lake City. Advance reservations are recommended for the trip from Cedar City to the park.

Once in the park, the longest hiking trail is the West Rim route, which begins near Zion Lodge. Another challenging trip involves hiking the Virgin River, an excursion best suited for low-water conditions.

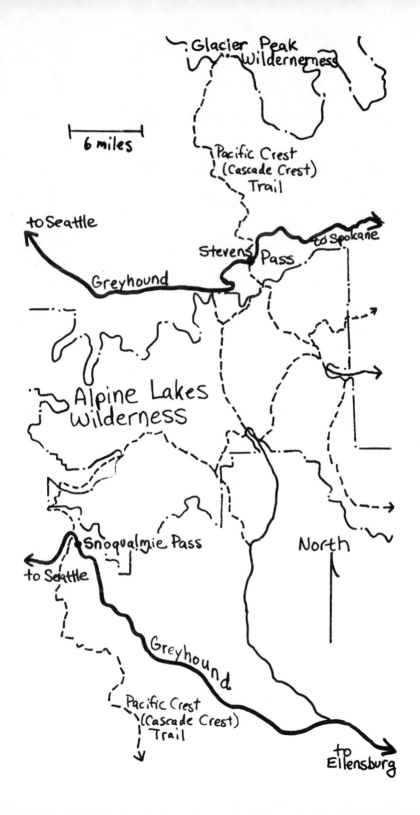

ALPINE LAKES WILDERNESS

Four hundred miles of trail with a variety of mountain terrain are available in this wilderness straddling the Cascade crest. Heavy snow provides opportunities for winter recreation, particularly on the colder, eastern side of the crest. The best public transportation access is from Stevens and Snoqualmie Passes. An excellent back-packing trip would be from one pass to the other using the Pacific Crest Trail.

Greyhound, enroute from Seattle to Spokane, has several daily flag stops in each direction at Stevens Pass. Snoqualmie Pass is also served several times daily by Greyhound on its Seattle to Ellensburg route.

In the past, several companies also have provided ski bus service from Seattle to the ski resorts located at each pass.

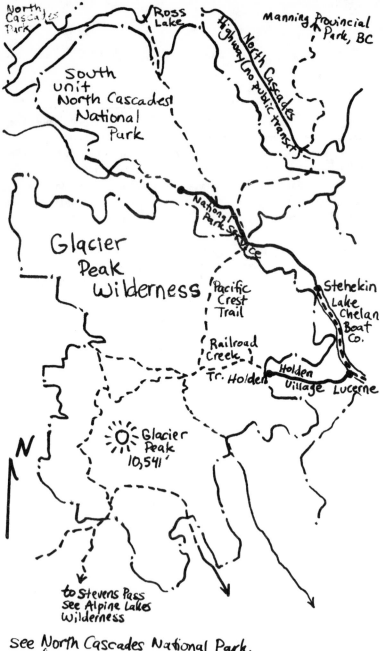

North
Cascades
Park

Ross
Lake

Manning Provincial
Park, BC

South
unit
North Cascades
National
Park

Highway (no public transit)

North Cascades

National Park Service

Glacier
Peak
Wilderness

Pacific
Crest
Trail

Stehekin
Lake
Chelan
Boat
Co.

Railroad
Creek

Tr. Holden

Holden
Village

Lucerne

N

Glacier
Peak
10,541'

to Stevens Pass
see Alpine Lakes
Wilderness

see North Cascades National Park
for more public transportation
information

6 miles

GLACIER PEAK WILDERNESS

The forgotten volcano of the Washington Cascades, Glacier
Peak is remote and mostly hidden from view for highway
travelers. Its very remoteness makes it attractive to
hikers and its 10,541 foot elevation makes it one of the
highest summits in Washington.

The best public transportation access into the wilderness
is via the Lake Chelan Boat Company ferry from Chelan
to Lucerne. Refer to the North Cascades National Park
entry for information on how to get to Chelan. From Lucerne,
a year round shuttle bus meets the ferry and travels to
Holden, where there is excellent hiking and snow travel
in season.

The shuttle bus is operated by Holden Village, a Lutheran
Church conference center.

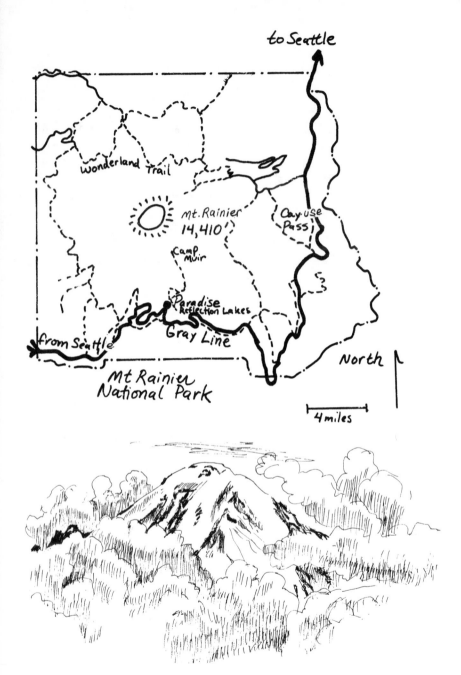

to Seattle

Wonderland Trail

Mt. Rainier
14,410'

Cayuse
Pass

Camp.
Muir

Paradise
Reflection Lakes

Gray Line

from Seattle

North

Mt Rainier
National Park

4 miles

Mt. Rainier

MT. RAINIER NATIONAL PARK

Mt. Rainier dominates the skyline in a large section of the state of Washington and it supports more glaciers than any other peak in the lower forty-eight states. Subalpine meadows, old growth forest and lakes are also part of the park landscape.

Public transportation is available from May to October using the Gray Lines tour bus that leaves Seattle daily, departing either from the Space Needle or the Westin Hotel. The bus circles the mountain via Stevens Canyon and Cayuse Pass and makes a stop at the Paradise Visitor Center as part of a one day tour. By prior arrangement, it is possible to leave the tour at Paradise or at several other trailheads on the bus route and rejoin it on another day for the return trip to Seattle. Early in the season, the bus route is sometimes changed from a loop trip around Mt. Rainier to a Seattle-Paradise return on the same route because of snow blocking roads.

From Paradise, hiking routes lead to the 10,000 foot elevation of Camp Muir and to the Reflection Lakes. The ninety mile Wonderland Trail that circles Mt. Rainier is another popular trip and is accessible from Paradise as well as other trailheads along the bus route.

North Cascades
National Park
Lake Chelan
National Recreation
Area

5 miles

Glacier Peak
Wilderness

Pacific Crest Trail

Pacific Crest

North

Cascade Pass

North
Cascades
National
Park

Cottonwood

Pacific
Crest Tr.

Bridge
Creek

High Bridge

National
Park
Shuttle

Lake
Chelan
Nat'l
Recreation
Area

Holden
Lake

Holden

Stehekin

Holden
Village

Lake
Chelan

boundaries
between
Park, wilderness,
national forest and
national recreation
area not
shown

2 miles

Moore

Lucerne

Lady of The
Lake to
25 mile Creek ↓ Chelan

NORTH CASCADES NATIONAL PARK
LAKE CHELAN NATIONAL RECREATION AREA

The key to enjoying this immense and beautiful complex
of wilderness in north central Washington is the freshwater
fjord, Lake Chelan, which threads its way into the North
Cascades and the ferry, Lady of the Lake, (operated by
the Lake Chelan Boat Company) that travels the fifty-five
miles from Chelan to Stehekin.

Empire Stages, enroute once daily from Wenatchee to Osoyoos,
B.C., stops in Chelan; Wenatchee and Osoyoos can both
be reached on Greyhound. Wenatchee is also served by AMTRAK.
Tell the Wenatchee to Chelan bus driver that you want
to be left off at the ferry terminal in Chelan. The bus-
ferry connection is tight and the boat dock is some distance
from the formal Chelan bus stop.

Once on the ferry towards Stehekin, the stops at Prince
Creek, Lucerne, Moore and Stehekin all offer fine opportunities for hiking and winter travel. The boat operates
four times weekly from October to May and daily in summer.
From mid-May through September, the National Park Service
operates the Stehekin Valley shuttle bus from Stehekin
to a number of trailheads within both North Cascades National
Park and Lake Chelan National Recreation Area. The shuttle
bus route crosses the Pacific Crest Trail at High Bridge.
This is currently the final public transportation access
point to the Crest Trail south of the Canadian border.

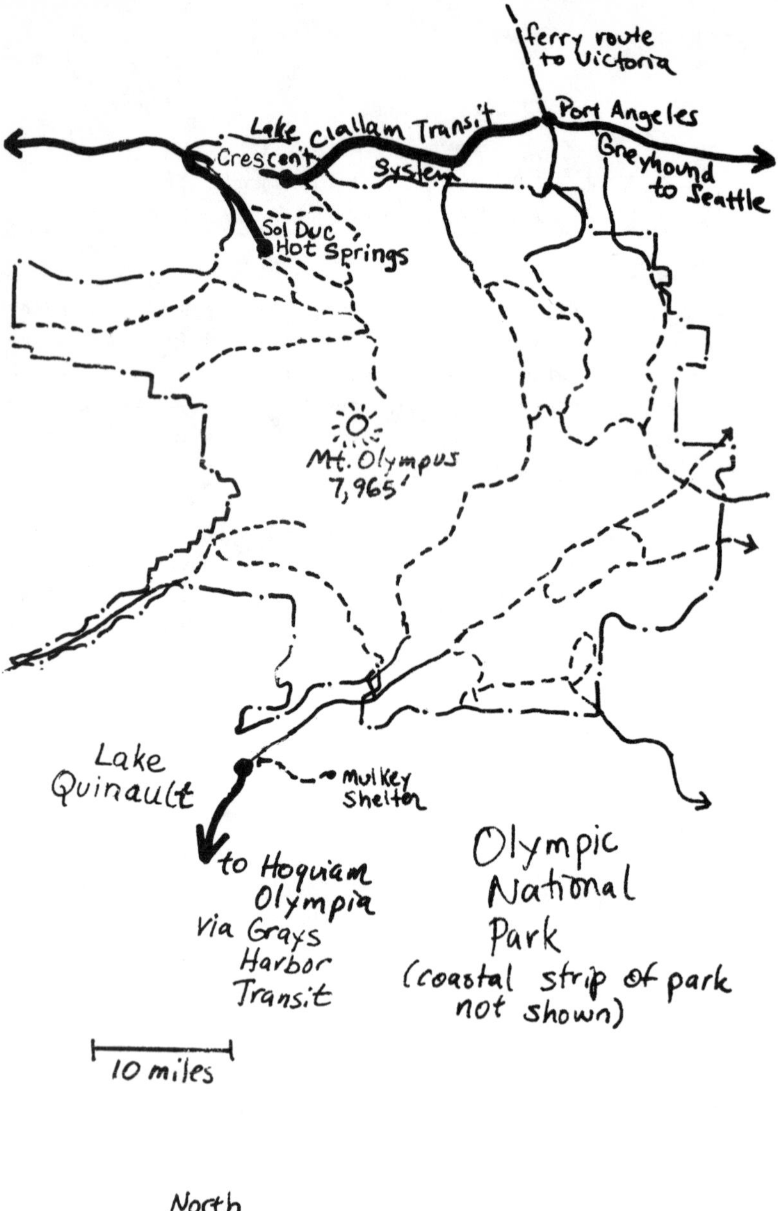

ferry route
to Victoria

Port Angeles

Lake Clallam Transit
System

Crescent

Greyhound
to Seattle

Sol Duc
Hot Springs

☼
Mt. Olympus
7,965'

Lake
Quinault

Mulkey
Shelter

to Hoquiam
Olympia
Via Grays
Harbor
Transit

Olympic
National
Park
(coastal strip of park
not shown)

10 miles

North

OLYMPIC NATIONAL PARK

Diverse Olympic National Park sprawls over glaciated mountains, maritime rainforests and unspoiled beaches. There are two possible ways to reach the park using public transportation.

Clallam Transit System (CTS) provides public transportation via Route 12 to Lake Crescent Lodge six days weekly from Port Angeles. A short distance east of the Lodge, at the Storm King Ranger Station, a trail leads past Marymere Falls onto Happy Lake Ridge. CTS Route 12 is extended twice daily to Sol Duc Hot Springs, with trails leading into Seven Lakes Basin and up over High Divide with its views of glacier clad Mt. Olympus. Port Angeles can be reached from Victoria, B.C. by the Black Ball Ferry and from Seattle by Greyhound and San Juan Airlines. CTS Route 24 serves the Airport six days weekly with hourly service and a transfer to the Lake Crescent bus can be made at Oak Street and Railroad Avenue. Current plans call for expansion of CTS routes to other communities and trailheads in and near the park, including two trailheads along the wilderness ocean front of the park. Contact the transit system for further information.

To get to Lake Quinault at the southwest corner of the park, take the Grays Harbor Transit bus, four times daily, except holidays, from the Olympia Greyhound depot to Hoquiam or Aberdeen. From 8 and K in Hoquiam or Rainier Bank in Aberdeen, take Grays Harbor Transit Route 60, service two to four times daily, except holidays, to Quinault. Olympia is served by Greyhound and Trailways.

Along the south shore of Lake Quinault are several campgrounds and a trail leading up Quinault Ridge five miles to Mulkey Shelter, within an undesignated wilderness area of Olympic National Forest.

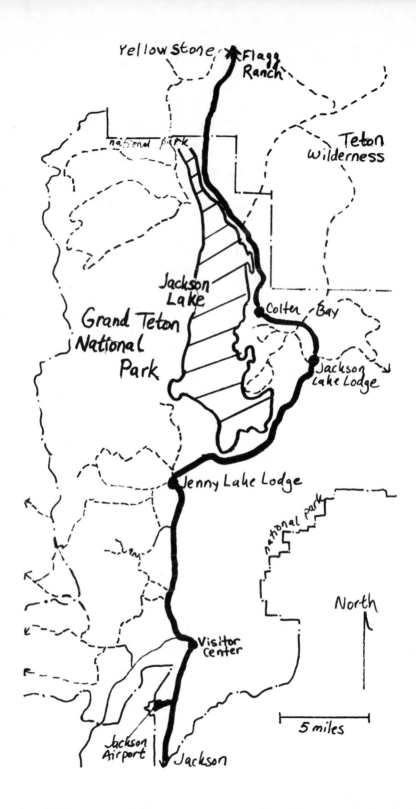

Yellowstone   Flagg Ranch

Teton Wilderness

national park

Jackson Lake

Grand Teton National Park

Colter Bay

Jackson Lake Lodge

Jenny Lake Lodge

national park

North

Visitor Center

5 miles

Jackson Airport

Jackson

GRAND TETON NATIONAL PARK

A summer trip to Yellowstone using public transportation can be combined easily with a trip to see the dramatic skyline of the Tetons, which rise precipitiously above Jackson Hole.

TWA Services, the Yellowstone concessionaire, provides daily summer service from Yellowstone (Canyon Village) to Jackson, with a stop at Jackson Lake Lodge. The Grand Teton Lodge Company also provides two daily trips from Jackson to Jackson Lake Lodge and they also meet all incoming scheduled flights at Jackson Airport. In addition, the lodge company has an hourly daytime shuttle bus from Jackson to Colter Bay Village. While there is hiking available at both Colter Bay Village and Jackson Lake Lodge, the best hiking in the park is closer to Jenny Lake Lodge, a stop on the twice daily Jackson-Jackson Lake Lodge route.

The Jenny Lake Lodge stop is made by request only, so check ahead with the Transportation Desk of the Grand Teton Lodge Co. for this and other travel arrangements within the park.

There are several means of reaching Jackson, including airline service. Rock Springs-Jackson Stage has a daily bus in the summer, three times weekly otherwise, from Rock Springs, which can be reached on Greyhound. Teton Stage Lines provides daily service in summer and three times weekly otherwise, from Idaho Falls (Greyhound connections). See the Palisades Backcountry Management Unit description under Idaho for additional hiking available along that bus route.

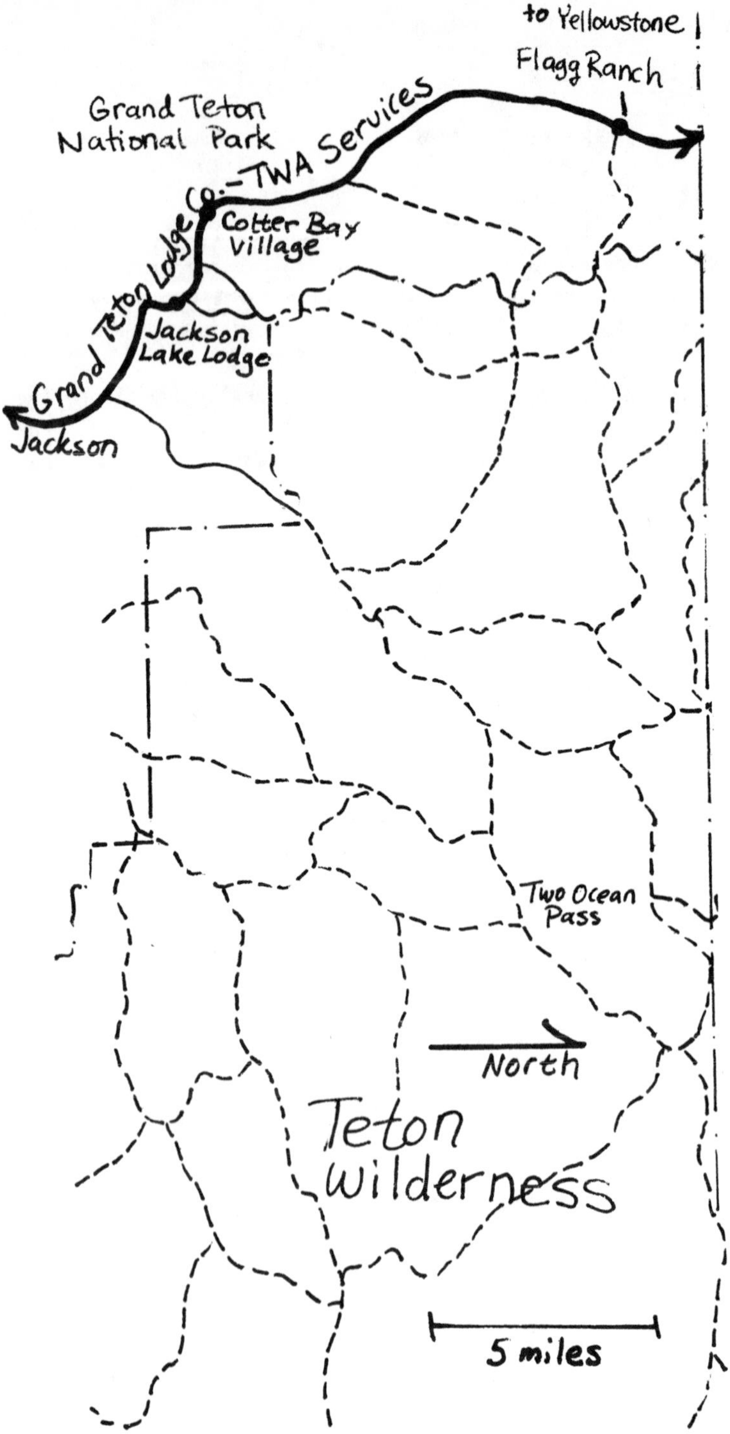

to Yellowstone

Flagg Ranch

Grand Teton
National Park

TWA Services

Cotter Bay
Village

Grand Teton Lodge Co.

Jackson
Lake Lodge

Jackson

Two Ocean
Pass

North

Teton
Wilderness

5 miles

TETON WILDERNESS

Straddling the Continental Divide and snug up against
Grand Teton and Yellowstone National Parks, the Teton
Wilderness is accessible using public transportation designed
to serve both parks.

TWA Services, the Yellowstone concessionaire, has scheduled
bus service once daily in the summer from Jackson to Canyon
Village in Yellowstone Park. The scheduled stop at Jackson
Lake Lodge and the flag stop at Flagg Ranch are both close
to Teton Wilderness trailheads. Grand Teton Lodge Company
operates a twice daily, summer only bus from Jackson to
Jackson Lake Lodge and also meets all scheduled incoming
flights at Jackson Airport (summer only).   Grand Teton
Lodge Co. buses stop on request at Jenny Lake Lodge (Grand
Teton Park trailheads), as well as Jackson Lake (park
and Teton Wilderness trailheads).

Jackson can be reached using Rock Springs-Jackson Stage
from Rock Springs, a community with Greyhound connections.
Jackson can also be reached using Teton Stage Lines from
Idaho Falls (Greyhound connections). See the Palisades
Backcountry Management Unit description (Idaho) for addi-
tional hiking suggestions along that bus route.

In the winter from December through March, daily bus service
is available to Flagg Ranch from Jackson, provided by
TWA Services. This route continues into Yellowstone Park
in the form of an over-snow vehicle. The route ends at
Old Faithful.

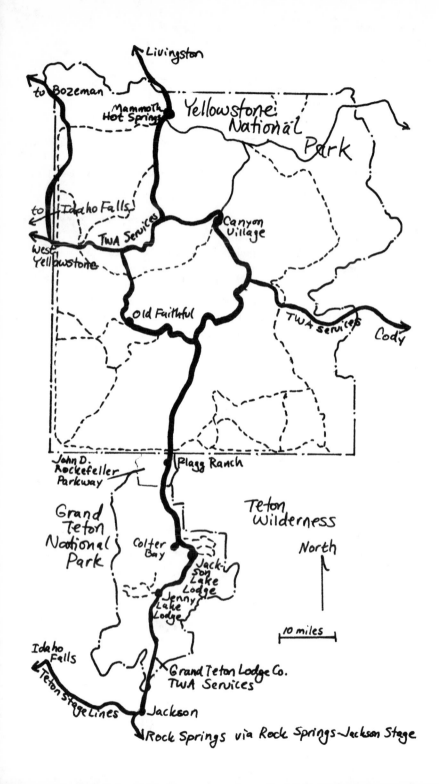

YELLOWSTONE NATIONAL PARK

Yellowstone is the largest unit of the National Park System south of Alaska; a park with geysers, scenery and abundant wildlife. It is probably as close to a "must-see" as any park in the United States.

The park is open year round to public transportation users and over-snow vehicles operated by TWA Services on the unplowed park roads have created the opportunity for more winter use of the park.

TWA Services has daily buses in the summer from Bozeman, Cody, Jackson, Livingston and West Yellowstone to Canyon Village. Yellowstone has about a thousand miles of trail and most of it is accessible using these buses.

In the winter peak season from December through March, over-snow vehicles provide service to Old Faithful from Flagg Ranch, Mammoth Hot Springs and West Yellowstone. Bus access to these starting points is provided by TWA Services from Bozeman (to Mammoth and West Yellowstone) and from Jackson (to Flagg Ranch). Reservations and pre-payment are required.

West Yellowstone can be reached by Greyhound and several airlines in the summer; Jackson has airline service and can be reached by Teton Stage Lines from Idaho Falls (Greyhound service) and Rock Springs-Jackson Stage from Rock Springs (Greyhound). Cody can be reached on Cody Bus Lines, a Trailways commission agent providing connections from Billings and Denver.

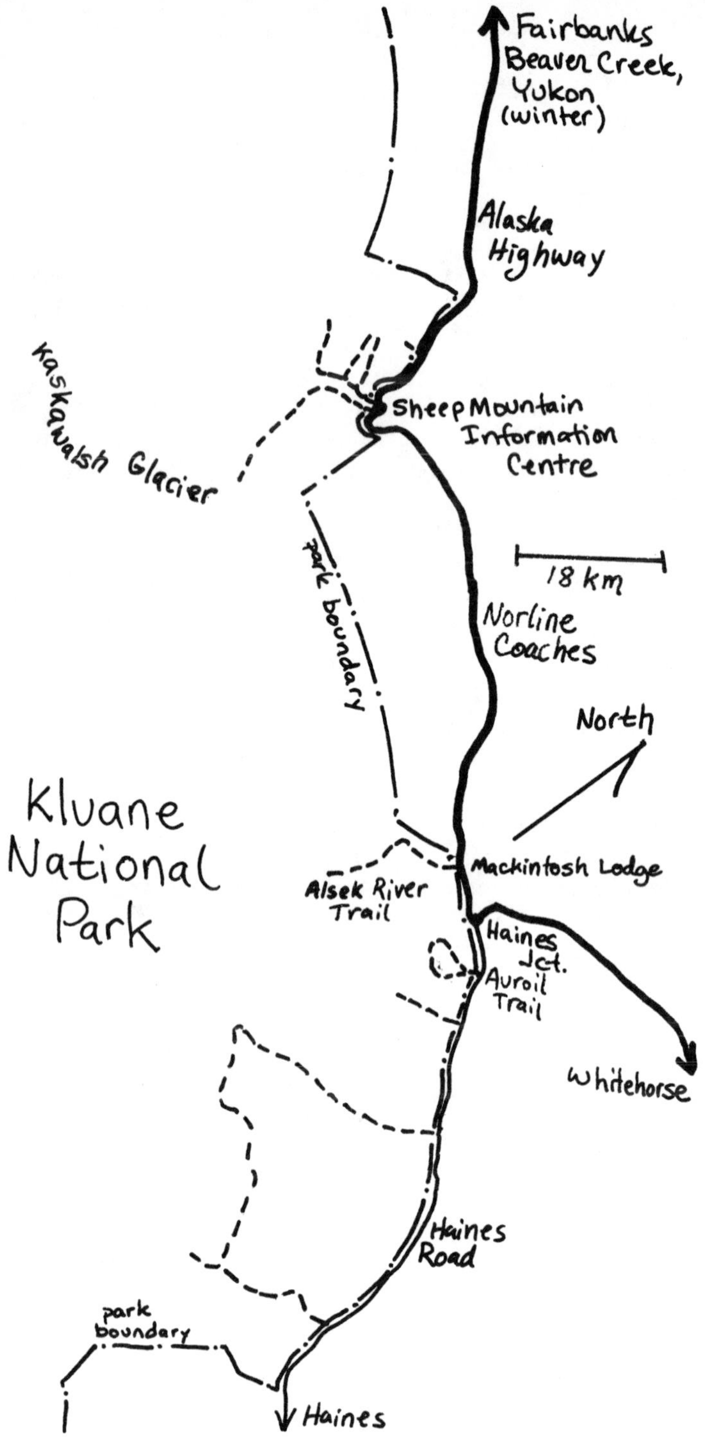

Fairbanks
Beaver Creek,
Yukon
(winter)

Alaska
Highway

Kaskawulsh Glacier

Sheep Mountain
Information
Centre

park boundary

18 km

Norline
Coaches

North

Kluane
National
Park

Alsek River
Trail

Mackintosh Lodge

Haines
Jct.

Auroil
Trail

Whitehorse

Haines
Road

park
boundary

Haines

KLUANE NATIONAL PARK

Within Kluane National Park are Canada's highest peaks. While the park is not as well known as Alaska's Denali National Park, the landscape is equally spectacular. Parks Canada is developing a trails network; the park visitor center in Haines Junction has a number of interesting exhibits and personnel there can provide the latest information on the trail system. There is mandatory registration for all overnight trips.

The park is bounded by two roads, the Alaska Highway, running northwest from Whitehorse, and the Haines Highway, connecting Haines (Alaska Marine Highway System ferries) to the Alaska Highway at Haines Junction. Both roads have had bus service, but there have been a number of changes in past years. Tourism Yukon (Box 2745, Whitehorse Y1A 5B9) keeps track of public transit within the Yukon and may be able to provide more up-to-date information.

Norline Coaches (Yukon) Ltd. has year round bus service through Haines Junction from Whitehorse, which can be reached on Canadian Coachways. It is also possible to reach Whitehorse from Skagway, another Alaska Marine Highway System ferry port. In the summer, the Norline Coaches bus continues twice weekly as far as Fairbanks, Alaska, in addition to other routes throughout the Yukon.

Within Kluane Park, the closest trails to Haines Junction are the Auroil Trail, about six km south, and the Alsek River Trail, about ten km west. The Alsek River Trail leads along an old mining road 24 km into the glacial headwaters of the Alsek River. Ask to get off at Mackintosh Lodge; the trail starts nearby. If other unscheduled stops can be arranged, there is another cluster of trails near the Sheep Mountain Information Center, operated by Parks Canada about 70 km west of Haines Junction.

D. Jacobson '84

TRANSPORTATION COMPANIES

This appendix lists in alphabetical order all transportation companies or agencies mentioned in the book. Contact them by mail or phone to confirm specific schedule and fare information. The addresses listed are mailing addresses and transit terminals may be located elsewhere.

Alaska Airlines
Seattle-Tacoma International Airport
Seattle, WA 98158
phone: consult local directory or travel agent

Alaska Marine Highway System
Pouch R
Juneau, AK 99811
(800) 551-7185 (Alaska)
(800) 544-2251 (lower 48)

Alaska Railroad
Pouch 7-2111
Anchorage, AK 99510
(907) 265-2685 (Anchorage)
(907) 456-4155 (Fairbanks)
(206) 442-5416 (Seattle)

Alaska - Yukon Motorcoaches
349 Wrangell Avenue
Anchorage, AK 99501
(907) 276-1305

Alberni Marine Transportation
PO Box 188
Port Alberni, British Columbia V9Y 7M7
(604) 723-8313

Albuquerque Sun-Tran
601 Yale Blvd. SE
Albuquerque, NM 87106
(505) 766-7830

Amador Stage Lines
213 13th Street
PO Box 15707
Sacramento, CA 95813
(916) 444-7880

AMTRAK
National Railroad Passenger Corporation
400 North Capitol Street NW
Washington, DC 20001
(800) USA-RAIL [(800) 872-7245]
in Canada: call VIA Rail
in Hawaii and Alaska: consult travel agent

Anchorage Public Transit
Customer Service Division
Pouch 6-650
Anchorage, AK 99502-0650
(907) 264-6543

British Columbia Railway
PO Box 8770
Vancouver, British Columbia V6B 1X4
(604) 987-6216 North Vancouver
(604) 564-9080 Prince George

Brown Lines
1410 East Edgewood Drive
Whitefish, MT 59937
(406) 257-1266

Calaveras Transit Company
PO Box 13
Vallecito, CA 95251
(209) 736-2743

Calgary Airporter
Brewster Transport, Ltd.
PO Box 1140
Banff, Alberta TOL OCO
(403) 762-2241 Banff
(403) 276-0766 Calgary

Canadian Coachways
222 1st Avenue SW
Calgary, Alberta T2P OA6
(403) 265-9111

Cariboo West Stage Lines
16 N. Broadway
Williams Lake, British Columbia V26 1B9
(604) 392-4283 Williams Lake
(604) 799-5467 Bella Coola

Carlsbad Cavern Coaches
contact T.N.M. & O. Coaches for more information

Catalina Cruises
PO Box 1948
San Pedro, CA 90733
(213) 514-3838

Catalina Express
Berth 95
PO Box 1391
San Pedro, CA 90733
(800) 468-2592 California
(213) 519-1212 San Pedro
(213) 510-1212 Avalon

Catalina Island Interior Shuttle Bus
213 Catalina Street
PO Box 2466
Avalon, CA 90704
(213) 510-2078

Catalina Passenger Service
Balboa Pavilion
400 Main Street
Balboa, CA 92661
(714) 673-5245

Clallam Transit System
2417 West 19th
Port Angeles, WA 98362
(206) 452-4511

Cody Bus Lines
PO Box 1480
Cody, WY 82414
(307) 587-4181

Color Country Tours
281 South Main Street
Cedar City, UT 84720
(801) 586-9916

Del Norte City and Public Bus
810 H Street
Crescent City, CA 95531
(707) 464-3069

Durango and Silverton Narrow Gauge Railroad
479 Main Avenue
Durango, CO 81301
(303) 247-2733

Eastern Sierra Shuttle
PO Box 792
Lone Pine, CA 93545
(619) 876-4435

Empire Stage Lines
PO Box 2205
910 W. Sprague
Spokane, WA 99210
(509) 624-4116

Estes Park Bus Company
PO Box 44
Estes Park, CO 80517
(303) 586-3301

Farwest Bus Lines
217 City Centre
Kitimat, British Columbia V8C 1T6
(604) 624-6400 Prince Rupert
(604) 635-6617 Terrace
(604) 632-3333 Kitimat
(604) 636-2414 Stewart

Glacier Park, Inc.
    May 15 to September 15:
    East Glacier, MT 59434
    (800) 332-9351 Montana
    (406) 226-5551

    September 15 to May 15:
    Greyhound Tower Mail Station 5185
    Phoenix, AZ 85077
    (602) 248-6000

Golden Empire Transit
1830 Golden State Avenue
Bakersfield, CA 93301
(805) 324-9874

Golden Gate Transit
Golden Gate Bridge, Highway and Transportation District
PO Box 9000, Presidio Station
San Francisco, CA 94129
(415) 332-6600
(415) 453-2100 Marin County
(707) 544-1323 Sonoma County

Grand Teton Lodge Company
PO Box 250
Moran, WY 83013
(307) 543-2811

Grayline of Alaska
dba White Pass and Yukon Motorcoaches
PO box 100479
Anchorage, AK 99510
(800) 544-2206 lower 48
(907) 983-2252

Gray Line of Seattle
2411 4th Avenue
Seattle, WA 98121
(206) 343-2000

Grays Harbor Transportation Authority
3000 Bay Avenue
Hoquiam, WA 98550
(800) 562-9730
(206) 532-2770

Greyhound Lines
Greyhound Tower
Phoenix, AZ 85077
phone: consult local directory

Greyhound Lines of Canada
222 1st Avenue
Calgary, Alberta T2P 0A6
(403) 265-9111

High Sierra Stages
The Rucksack
1043 S. Mooney Blvd.
Visalia, CA 93277
(209) 732-4404

Holden Village
Chelan, WA 98816
(509) 687-3644 answering service at 25 Mile Creek

Humboldt Transit System
6700 N. Highway 101
Eureka, CA 95501
(707) 443-0826

Intermountain Transportation Company
7-9 Main Street
Anaconda, MT 59711
(406) 563-5246

Kern Rural Transit Systems
6201 Schirra Court
Bakersfield, CA 93309
(805) 325-5273

Lake Chelan Boat Company
PO Box 186
1418 Woodin Avenue
Chelan, WA 98816
(509) 682-2224

Lake O'Hara Lodge
      June to September:
      PO Box 55
      Lake Louise, Alberta T0L 1E0
      (403) 343-6418

      September to May:
      PO Box 1677
      Banff, Alberta T0L 0C0
      (403) 762-2118

Las Vegas - Tonopah - Reno Stage Line
2915 Sunrise Avenue
PO Box 42130
Las Vegas, NV 89116
(702) 384-1230

Long Beach Transit
1300 Gardenia Avenue
Long Beach, CA 90813
(213) 591-2301

Lost Trail Stage Line
Route 1, Box 189
Salmon, ID 83467
(208) 756-2870 Salmon
(208) 756-3470 Salmon
(406) 721-7204 Missoula

MarkAir
PO Box 6769
6441 South Air Park Place
Anchorage, AK 99502
(800) 426-6784

Maverick Coach Lines
1375 Vernon Drive
Vancouver, British Columbia V6A 3V4
(604) 255-1171

Monterey - Salinas Transit
One Ryan Ranch Road
Monterey, CA 93940
(408) 899-2555
(408) 424-7695

Mt. Lassen Motor Transit
Route 2, Box 2931
Red Bluff, CA 96080
(916) 529-2722

Nava - Hopi Tours
PO Box 339
Flagstaff, AZ 86001
(602) 774-5003

Norline Coaches (Yukon), Ltd.
3211 A 3rd Street
Whitehorse, Yukon Y1A 1G6
(403) 663-3355

Northeast Rural Bus System
San Diego County Department of Public Works
Building 2, 5555 Overland Avenue
San Diego, CA 92123
(619) 765-0145 or Zenith 7-0145

Orient Stage Lines
Box 46, R.R. 2
Port Alberni, British Columbia V9Y 7L6
(604) 723-6924

The Outdoorsman
197 N. Main Street
Bishop, CA 93514
(619) 873-3015

Peerless Stages
228 Broadway
Oakland, CA 94607
(415) 444-2900 Oakland
(408) 423-1800 Santa Cruz

Pitkin County Bus System
Pitkin County Government
Sardy Field
Aspen, CO 81611
(303) 925-4326

Resort Bus Lines
1223 NE First Street
Bend, OR 97701
(503) 389-7755

Rock Springs – Jackson Stage
2016 Carson
Rock Springs, WY 82901
(307) 362-6161 Rock Springs; (307) 733-3133 Jackson

Santa Barbara Metropolitan Transit
550 East Cota
Santa Barbara, CA 93103
(805) 683-3702

Santa Cruz Metropolitan Transit
230 Walnut Avenue
Santa Cruz, CA 95060
(408) 425-8600

Sequoia and Kings Canyon Hospitality Service
Giant Forest Lodge
Sequoia National Park, CA 93262
(209) 565-3373

Seward Bus Line
PO Box 1338
Seward, AK 99664
(907) 224-3608 Seward; (907) 276-4309 Anchorage

Siskiyou Transit and General Express
Siskiyou County Department of Public Works
305 Butte Street
Yreka, CA 96097
(916) 842-3531 ext. 215

Sky West Airlines
Municipal Airport, PO Box T
St. George, UT 84770
(801) 628-2655

Stockton Metropolitan Transit
1533 E. Lindsay
Stockton, CA 95205
(209) 943-1111

Southern California Rapid Transit District (RTD)
Customer Relations
425 S. Main Street
Los Angeles, CA 90013
(818) 246-2593 Pasadena
(213) 626-4455 Los Angeles

Teton Stage Lines
1425 Lindsay Blvd.
Idaho Falls, ID 83402
(208) 529-8036

Timberline Lodge
Timberline, OR 97028
(503) 226-7979
(503) 272-3311

T.N.M. & O. Coaches
1313 13th Street
PO Box 1800
Lubbock, TX 79408
(806) 763-5389

Trailways
    National Trailways Bus System
    1200 Eye Street NW
    Washington, DC 20005

    Trailways Lines, Inc.
    1500 Jackson Street
    Dallas, TX 75201

phone: consult local directory

Tucson Sun-Trans
4220 S. Park, Building 10
PO Box 26765
Tucson, AZ 85726
(602) 792-9222

TWA Services
Gardiner, MT 59030 or Yellowstone National Park, WY 82190
(307) 344-7901

Utah Transit Authority
Customer Service
3600 South 700 West
PO Box 31810
Salt Lake City, UT 84131
(801) 263-3737

Vancouver Island Coach Lines
710 Douglas Street
Victoria, British Columbia V8W 2B3
(604) 385-4411

VIA Rail Canada
PO Box 8116
1801 McGill College, Floor 13
Montréal, Quebec H3C 3N3
phone: consult directory (Canada)
       call AMTRAK (800) USA-RAIL (contiguous U.S.)
       consult travel agent (elsewhere)

Wallowa Valley Stage Line
PO Box 156
Lostine, OR 97857
(503) 569-2284

White Mountain Lines
PO Box 460
Show Low, AZ 85901
(602) 537-4539

Yosemite Transportation System
Reservations Office
5410 E. Home Avenue
Fresno, CA 93727
(209) 252-4848 Fresno
(209) 722-0366 Merced

ADMINISTRATIVE AGENCIES
ALASKA

Chugach National Forest
2221 E. Northern Lights Blvd. #238
Anchorage, AK 99508
(907) 279-5541

Chugach State Park
2601 Commercial Drive
Anchorage, AK 99501
(907) 279-3413

Denali National Park and Preserve
PO Box 9
Denali Park, AK 99755

Denali State Park
Mat-Su District
Alaska Division of Parks
PO Box 182
Palmer, AK 99645

Glacier Bay National Park and Preserve
Gustavus, AK 99826
(907) 697-3341

Katmai National Park and Preserve
PO Box 7
King Salmon, AK 99613
(907) 246-3305

Klondike Gold Rush National Historic Park
PO Box 517
Skagway, AK 99840

Tongass National Forest
Federal Building
Ketchikan, AK 99901
(907) 225-3101

PO Box 1980
Sitka, AK 99835

PO Box 309
Petersburg, AK 99833

ALBERTA

Banff National Park
PO Box 900
Banff, Alberta TOL OCO
(403) 762-3324

Jasper National Park
PO Box 10
Jasper, Alberta TOE 1EO
(403) 852-4401

Waterton Lakes National Park
Waterton Park, Alberta TOK 2MO
(403) 859-2445

ARIZONA

Grand Canyon National Park
PO Box 129
Grand Canyon, AZ 86023
(602) 638-2474 (Backcountry Reservation Office)

Mazatzal Wilderness
Tonto National Forest
102 S. 28th Street
PO Box 13705
Phoenix, AZ 85002
(602) 261-3205

Pauite Primitive Area
Arizona Strip District
Bureau of Land Management
196 E. Tabernacle
PO Box 250
St. George, UT 84770
(801) 673-3545

Pusch Ridge Wilderness
Coronado National Forest
Federal Building
301 West Congress
Tucson, AZ 85701
(602) 792-6483

BRITISH COLUMBIA

Alaska Highway/British Columbia
Peace River/Alaska Highway Tourist Association
9223 100th St.
Fort St. John, British Columbia V1J 4J3
(604) 785-2544

Parks and Outdoor Recreation Division
1019 Wharf Street
Victoria, British Columbia V8W 2Y9
(604) 387-1696

Garibaldi Provincial Park
Parks and Outdoor Recreation Division
1019 Wharf Street
Victoria, British Columbia V8W 2Y9
(604) 387-1696

Glacier National Park
PO Box 350
Revelstoke, British Columbia V0E 2S0
(604) 837-5155

Howe Sound
Southwestern British Columbia Tourist Association
PO Box 94449
#2-5760 Minoru Blvd.
Richmond, British Columbia V6Y 2A8
(604) 270-6801

Kootenay National Park
PO Box 220
Radium Hot Springs, British Columbia V0A 1M0
(604) 347-9615

Manning Provincial Park
Parks and Outdoor Recreation Division
1019 Wharf Street
Victoria, British Columbia V8W 2Y9
(604) 387-1696

District Manager
Manning Park, British Columbia V0X 1R0
(604) 840-8836

Mt. Revelstoke National Park
PO Box 350
Revelstoke, British Columbia V0E 2S0
(604) 837-5155

Mt. Robson Provincial Park (described under Jasper, Alberta)
Parks and Outdoor Recreation Division
1019 Wharf Street
Victoria, British Columbia V8W 2Y9
(604) 387-1696

Park Supervisor
PO Box 579
Valemount, British Columbia V0E 2Z0
(604) 566-4325

Pacific Rim National Park
PO Box 280
Ucluelet, British Columbia V0R 3A0
(604) 726-4212

Portland Canal
Stewart Historical Society and Tourist Information Centre
PO Box 690
Stewart, British Columbia V0T 1W0
(604) 636-2568

British Columbia Yellowhead 16 Tourist Association
PO Box 1030
1283 Main Street
Smithers, British Columbia V0J 2N0
(604) 847-5227

Tweedsmuir Provincial Park
Parks and Outdoor Recreation Division
1019 Wharf Street
Victoria, British Columbia V8W 2Y9
(604) 387-1696

Park Supervisor, South Tweedsmuir Park
PO Box 126
Bella Coola, British Columbia V0T 1C0
(604) Williams Lake Radio Operator, Tweedsmuir Park N692224

Yoho National Park
Field, British Columbia V0A 1G0
(604) 343-6324

CALIFORNIA

Angeles National Forest
150 S. Los Robles Avenue
Pasadena, CA 91101
(818) 577-0050 or (213) 684-0350 (from Los Angeles)

Anza-Borrego Desert State Park
Borrego Springs, CA 92004
(619) 767-5311

Big Basin Redwoods State Park
21600 Big Basin Way
Boulder Creek, CA 95006
(408) 338-6132

Catalina Island
Los Angeles County Department of Parks and Recreation
PO Box 1133
Avalon, CA 90704
(213) 510-0688 (for camping at Little Harbor, Black Jack and
              Bird Park near Avalon)

Catalina Cove and Camp Agency
PO Box 1566
Avalon, CA 90704
(213) 510-0303 (for camping at Parson's Landing and Little
              Fisherman's Cove)

Death Valley National Monument
Death Valley, CA 92328
(619) 786-2331

Desolation Wilderness
Eldorado National Forest
100 Forni Road
Placerville, CA 95667
(916) 622-5061

Domeland Wilderness
Sequoia National Forest
900 W. Grand Avenue
Porterville, CA 93257
(209) 784-1500

Emigrant Wilderness
Stanislaus National Forest
175 South Fairview Lane
Sonora, CA 95370
(209) 532-3671

Golden Gate National Recreation Area
Fort Mason
San Francisco, CA 94123
(415) 556-0560

Humboldt Redwoods State Park
PO Box 100
Weott, CA 95571
(707) 946-2311

John Muir Wilderness
Inyo National Forest
873 N. Main Street
Bishop, CA 93514
(619) 873-5841

Lassen Volcanic National Park
Mineral, CA 96063
(916) 595-4444

Mokelumne Wilderness
El Dorado National Forest
100 Forni Road
Placerville, CA 95667
(916) 622-5061

Point Reyes National Seashore
Point Reyes, CA 94956
(415) 663-1092

Redwood National Park
1111 2nd Street
Crescent City, CA 95531
(707) 464-6101

Santa Ynez Mountains
Los Padres National Forest
42 Aero Camino
Goleta, CA 93017
(805) 968-1578

Sequoia and Kings Canyon National Parks
Three Rivers, CA 93271
(209) 565-3364 or (209) 335-2315

Siskiyou Mountains
Klamath National Forest
1312 Fairlane Road
Yreka, CA 96097
(916) 842-6131

Ventana Wilderness
Los Padres National Forest
42 Aero Camino
Goleta, CA 93017

Yosemite National Park
Yosemite National Park, CA 95389
(209) 372-4461

COLORADO

Big Blue Wilderness
Uncompahgre National Forest
2250 Highway 50
Delta, CO 81416
(303) 874-7691

Eagles Nest Wilderness
301 S. Howes
PO Box 1366
Fort Collins, CO 80522
(303) 482-5155

Holy Cross Wilderness
White River National Forest
PO Box 948, Old Federal Building
Glenwood Springs, CO 81601
(303) 945-2521

Lost Creek and Mt. Evans Wildernesses
Pike National Forest
1920 Valley Drive
Pueblo, CO 81008
(303) 852-5941

Maroon Bells - Snowmass Wilderness
same agency address as Holy Cross Wilderness, above

Rocky Mountain National Park
Estes Park, CO 80517
(303) 586-2371 (Backcountry Office)

Weminuche Wilderness
Rio Grande National Forest
1803 West Highway 160
Monte Vista, CO 81144
(303) 852-5941

San Juan National Forest
701 Camino del Rio
Durango, CO 81301
(303) 247-4874

IDAHO

Palisades Backcountry Management Area
Targhee National Forest
420 North Bridge Street
St. Anthony, ID 83445
(208) 624-3151

Panhandle National Forest
1201 Ironwood Drive
Coeur d'Alene, ID 83815
(208) 765-7561

West Bigholes
Salmon National Forest
Forest Service Building
PO Box 729
Salmon, ID 83467
(208) 756-2215

MONTANA

Cabinet Mountains Wilderness
Kootenai National Forest
Box AS
West Highway 2
Libby, MT 59923
(406) 293-6211

Glacier National Park
West Glacier, MT 59936
(406) 888-5441

Spanish Peaks Wilderness
Gallatin National Forest
Federal Building
PO Box 130
Bozeman, MT 59715
(406) 587-5271

NEW MEXICO

Carlsbad Caverns National Park
3225 National Parks Highway
Carlsbad, NM 88220
(505) 785-2232

Sandia Mountain Wilderness
Cibola National Forest
10308 Candelaria NE
Albuquerque, NM 87112
(505) 766-2185

                              OREGON

Columbia River Gorge
Mt. Hood National Forest
2955 NW Division
Gresham, OR 97030
(503) 667-0511

Diamond Peak Wilderness
Deschutes National Forest
211 NE Revere St.
Bend, OR 97701
(503) 382-6922

Eagle Cap Wilderness
Wallowa-Whitman National Forest
PO Box 907
Federal Office Building
Baker, OR 97401
(503) 523-6391

Mt. Hood Wilderness
Mt. Hood National Forest
2955 NW Division
Gresham, OR 97030
(503) 667-0511

Mt. Jefferson Wilderness
Mt. Washington Wilderness
Deschutes National Forest
211 NE Revere St.
Bend, OR 97701
(503) 382-6922

Willamette National Forest
PO Box 10607
211 East 7th Avenue
Eugene, OR 97401
(503) 882-7761

Oregon Coast Trail
State Parks and Recreation Branch
525 Trade Street SE
Salem, OR 97310
(503) 378-6305

Oregon Dunes National Recreation Area
Siuslaw National Forest
855 Highway Avenue
Reedsport, OR 97467
(503) 271-3611

U T A H

Bryce Canyon National Park
Bryce Canyon, UT 84717
(801) 834-5322

Wasatch Range
Wasatch and Cache National Forests
8226 Federal Building
125 South State Street
Salt Lake City, UT 84138
(801) 524-5030

Uinta National Forest
PO Box 1428
88 West 100 North
Provo, UT 84603
(801) 377-5780

Zion National Park
Springdale, UT 84767
(801) 772-3256

WASHINGTON

Alpine Lakes Wilderness
Mt. Baker-Snoqualmie National Forest
1022 First Avenue
Seattle, WA 98104
(206) 442-0171

Wenatchee National Forest
PO Box 811
301 Yakima Street
Wenatchee, WA 98801
(509) 662-4335

Glacier Peak Wilderness
Wenatchee National Forest
PO Box 811
301 Yakima Street
Wenatchee, WA 98801
(509) 662-4335

Mt. Rainier National Park
Ashford, WA 98304
(206) 569-2211

North Cascades National Park
Lake Chelan National Recreation Area
Sedro Wooley, WA 98284
(206) 873-4590

Olympic National Park
600 East Park Avenue
Port Angeles, WA 98267
(206) 452-9235

Pasayten Wilderness (described under Manning Provincial Park,
                     British Columbia)
Okanogan National Forest
PO Box 950
1240 2nd Avenue South
Okanogan, WA 98840
(509) 422-2704

WYOMING

Grand Teton National Park
Moose, WY 83012
(307) 733-2880

Teton Wilderness
Bridger-Teton National Forest
Forest Service Building
PO Box 1888
Jackson, WY 83001
(307) 733-2752

Yellowstone National Park
Yellowstone National Park, WY 82190
(307) 344-7381

THE YUKON

Kluane National Park
Haines Junction, Yukon Y0B 1L0
(403) 634-2251

BIBLIOGRAPHY

While the following list is by no means complete, it
does contain a large number of the hiking guides currently
in print that feature areas in this book. Many bookstores
will special order titles they do not stock or you can
write directly to the publisher. Publisher addresses
either follow mention of the book or are contained in
Appendix IV. Appendix IV also contains addresses of
several mail order services that specialize in outdoor
or travel books.

ALASKA

Alaska's Parklands: The Complete Guide by Nancy Simmerman.
The Mountaineers, Seattle.

55 Ways to Wilderness in Southcentral Alaska by Nancy
Simmerman and Helen Nienheuser. The Mountaineers, Seattle.

The Alaska – Yukon Handbook by David Stanley. Moon Publica-
tions, PO Box 1696, Chico, CA 95927.

Alaska – A Travel Survival Guide by Jim DuFresne. Lonely
Planet Travel Guide Series (Australia). Distributed by
Hippocrene Books, 171 Madison Avenue, New York, NY 10016.

The Milepost Guide. Updated yearly by Alaska Northwest
Publishing Co., 130 Second Avenue S., Edmonds, WA 98020.

Adventuring in Alaska: The Ultimate Travel Guide to the
Great Land by Peggy Wayburn. Sierra Club Books, San Francisco.

Juneau's Trails by Glen Gray. Published by Chatham Area,
Tongass National Forest, PO Box 1049, Juneau, AK 99802.

Sitka Trail Guide. City and Borough of Sitka, Parks and
Recreation Committee, PO Box 79, Sitka, AK 99835.

ALBERTA

95 Hikes in the Canadian Rockies: Banff, Kootenay and Assiniboine Parks by Vicky Spring and Gordon King. The Mountaineers, Seattle.

94 Hikes in the Canadian Rockies: Yoho, Jasper, Mt. Robson and Willmore Wilderness Parks by Vicky Spring and Dee Urbick. The Mountaineers, Seattle.

The Complete Guide to Backpacking in Canada by Eliot Katz. East Woods Press, Charlotte.

ARIZONA

Grand Canyon Treks, Grand Canyon Treks II and Grand Canyon Treks III by Harvey Butchart. La Siesta Press, Glendale, CA.

Grand Canyon National Park: Guide and Reference Book by C. McAdams. Pruett Publishing, Denver.

Arizona Trails by David Mazel. Wilderness Press, Berkeley

Grand Canyon and Havasu by Douglas Stevens and Herschel Scott. Poverty Hill Press, PO Box 7376, Reno, NV 89510.

A Guide to the South Kaibab Trail by Rose Houk. Grand Canyon Natural History Association, Grand Canyon National Park, AZ 86023

BRITISH COLUMBIA

Exploring Manning Park by Andrew Harcombe and Robert Cyca. The Mountaineers, Seattle.

103 Hikes in Southwestern British Columbia by David and Mary Macaree. The Mountaineers, Seattle.

109 Hikes in B.C.'s Lower Mainland by David and Mary
Macaree. The Mountaineers, Seattle.

94 Hikes in the Canadian Rockies: Yoho, Jasper, Mt. Robson
and Willmore Wilderness Parks by Dee Urbick and Vicky
Spring. The Mountaineers, Seattle.

Hiking Trails of the Sunshine Coast by Pam Barnsley,
et al. Harbour Publishing, Madeira Park, B.C./Signpost
Books, Edmonds, WA.

West Coast Trail and Nitinat Lakes by Sierra Club of
B.C. Signpost Books, Edmonds, WA.

Crosscountry Ski Routes: British Columbia by Richard
and Rochelle Wright. Signpost Books, Edmonds, WA.

CALIFORNIA

High Sierra Hiking Guide Series by various authors. Wilderness Press, Berkeley.

The Pacific Crest Trail, Volume 1: California by Schaffer,
et al. Wilderness Press, Berkeley.

Starr's Guide to the John Muir Trail and the High Sierra
Region by Walter A. Starr, edited by Douglas Robinson.
Sierra Club Books, San Francisco.

Timberline Country: The Sierra High Route by Steve Roper.
Sierra Club Books, San Francisco.

The Sierra Club Guide to the Natural Areas of California
by John and Jane Greverus Perry. Sierra Club Books, San
Francisco.

To Walk With a Quiet Mind: Hikes in the Woodlands, Parks
and Beaches of the San Francisco Bay Area by Nancy Olmsted.
Sierra Club Books, San Francisco.

Outdoor Guide to the San Francisco Bay Area by Dorothy Whitnah. Wilderness Press, Berkeley.

Point Reyes by Dorothy Whitnah. Wilderness Press, Berkeley.

Ski Touring in California by Dave Beck. Wilderness Press, Berkeley.

Trails of the Angeles by John W. Robinson. Wilderness Press, Berkeley.

The Tahoe - Yosemite Trail by Thomas Winnett. Wilderness Press, Berkeley.

The Tahoe Sierra by Jeffrey Schaffer. Wilderness Press, Berkeley.

Lassen Volcanic National Park by Jeffrey Schaffer. Wilderness Press, Berkeley.

Yosemite National Park by Jeffrey Schaffer. Wilderness Press, Berkeley.

The John Muir Trail by Thomas Winnett. Wilderness Press, Berkeley.

Desolation Wilderness and the South Lake Tahoe Basin by Jeffrey Schaffer. Wilderness Press, Berkeley.

Sierra North by Winnett and Winnett. Wilderness Press, Berkeley.

Sierra South by Winnett and Winnett. Wilderness Press, Berkeley.

Marble Mountain Wilderness by David Green. Wilderness Press, Berkeley.

The Anza-Borrego Desert Region by Lindsay and Lindsay. Wilderness Press, Berkeley.

Sierra Club Guide to the National Parks of the Pacific Southwest and Hawaii by Stewart, et al. Sierra Club Books, San Francisco.

COLORADO

Hiking Trails of Central Colorado by Bob Martin. Pruett Publishing, Boulder.

Rocky Mountain Trails by Louis Kenofer. Pruett Publishing, Boulder.

Hiking Trails of Southwestern Colorado by Paul Pixler. Pruett Publishing, Boulder.

Rocky Mountain National Park Hiking Trails by Kent and Donna Dannen. East Woods Press, Charlotte.

IDAHO

The Hiker's Guide to Idaho by Jackie Maughan. Falcon Press, Billings.

North Idaho Hiking Trails by Sheldon Bluestein. Challenge Expedition Co. PO Box 1852, Boise, ID 83701

MONTANA

The Nordic Skier's Guide to Montana by Elaine Sedlack. Falcon Press, Billings.

Hiker's Guide to Glacier National Park by Dick and Sharon Nelson. Tecolote Press, PO Box 188, Glenwood, NM 88039.

Hiker's Guide to Montana by Bill Schneider. Falcon Press, Billings.

NEW MEXICO

Guide to the New Mexico Mountains by Herbert Ungnade. University of New Mexico Press, Albuquerque.

Hikers and Climbers Guide to the Sandia Mountains by Mike Hill. University of New Mexico Press, Albuquerque.

Hiking the Southwest: Arizona, New Mexico and West Texas by Dave Ganci. Sierra Club Books, San Francisco.

OREGON

Cross-Country Ski Routes of Oregon's Cascades: Mt. Hood-Bend by Klindt Vielbig. The Mountaineers, Seattle.

The Sierra Club Guide to the Natural Areas of Oregon and Washington by John and Jane Greverus Perry. Sierra Club Books, San Francisco.

60 Hiking Trails, Central Oregon Cascades by Don and Roberta Lowe. Touchstone Press, Beaverton, OR.

62 Hiking Trails, Northern Oregon Cascades by Don and Roberta Lowe. Touchstone Press, Beaverton, OR.

35 Hiking Trails, Columbia River Gorge by Don and Roberta Lowe. Touchstone Press, Beaverton, OR.

The Pacific Crest Trail: Oregon - Washington by Schaffer, et al. Wilderness Press, Berkeley.

UTAH

The Hiker's Guide to Utah by Dave Hall. Falcon Press, Billings.

Wasatch Trails, Volume 1, by Betty Bottcher and Mel Davis. Wasatch Publishers, Salt Lake City.

Wasatch Trails, Volume II, by Daniel Geery. Wasatch Publishers, Salt Lake City.

Wasatch Tours by Alexis Kelner and David Hanscom. Wasatch Publishers, Salt Lake City.

Sierra Club Guide to the National Parks of the Desert Southwest by Stewart, et al. Sierra Club Books, San Francisco.

Wasatch Hiking Map. University of Utah Press, Salt Lake City, UT 84112.

WASHINGTON

Cross-country Ski Trails of Washington's Cascades and Olympics by Tom Kirkendall and Vicky Spring. The Mountaineers, Seattle.

Snow Trails: Ski and Snowshoe Routes in the Cascades by Gene Prater. The Mountaineers, Seattle.

102 Hikes in the Alpine Lakes, South Cascades and Olympics by Harvey Manning and Bob and Ira Spring. The Mountaineers, Seattle.

101 Hikes in the North Cascades by Harvey Manning and Bob and Ira Spring. The Mountaineers, Seattle.

50 Hikes in Mt. Rainier National Park by Harvey Manning and Bob and Ira Spring. The Mountaineers, Seattle.

Olympic Mountains Trail Guide by Robert L. Wood. The Mountaineers, Seattle.

Stehekin: A Guide to the Enchanted Valley by Fred Darvil. Signpost Books, Edmonds, WA.

Hiking the North Cascades by Fred Darvil. Sierra Club Books, San Francisco.

WYOMING

Beyond the Tetons by Ralph Maughan. Pruett Publishing, Boulder.

Wyoming Hiking Trails by Tom and Sanse Sudduth. Pruett Publishing, Boulder.

Yellowstone National Park: Guide and Reference Book by Cliff McAdams. Falcon Press, Billings.

Hiking the Teton Backcountry by Paul Lawrence. Sierra Club Books, San Francisco.

Hiking the Yellowstone Backcountry by Oroville E. Bach Sierra Club Books, San Francisco.

Mimulus caespitosa
Weminuche Wilderness

HIKING GUIDE PUBLISHERS

East Woods Press
429 East Boulevard
Charlotte, NC 28203

Falcon Press
PO Box 279
Billings, MT 59103

Harbour Publishing
PO Box 119
Madeira Park, B.C. VON 2H0

La Siesta Press
PO Box 406
Glendale, CA 91209

The Mountaineers
715 Pike Street
Seattle, WA 98101

Pruett Publishing
2928 Pearl Street
Boulder, CO 80301

Sierra Club Books
2034 Fillmore Street
San Francisco, CA 94115

Signpost Books
8912 192nd SW
Edmonds, WA 98020

Touchstone Press
ordering: TMS Book Service
PO Box 1504
Beaverton, OR 97075

University of New Mexico Press
Albuquerque, NM 87131

Wasatch Publishers
4647 Idlewild Road
Salt Lake City, UT 84124

Wilderness Press
2440 Bancroft Way
Berkeley, CA 94704-1676

MAIL ORDER FIRMS SPECIALIZING IN TRAVEL AND/OR OUTDOOR BOOKS

The Best Choice
PO Box 13
Hershey, PA 17033
(800) 233-2175
(800) 222-1934

Book Passage
57 Post Street, Suite 401
San Francisco, CA 94104
(415) 982-7866

Books to Go
14755 Ventura Blvd.
Sherman Oaks, CA 91403

The Complete Traveller Bookstore
199 Madison Avenue
New York, NY 10016
(212) 685-9007

Forsyth Travel Library
PO Box 2975
9154 W. 57th Street
Shawnee Mission, KS 66201
(913) 384-3440

Great Expeditions Books
PO Box 46499
Station G
Vancouver, British Columbia V6R 4G7

Nomadic Books
PO Box 31529
Seattle, WA 98103

Take a Walk
PO Box 1463
Palo Alto, CA 94301

Traveller's Bookstore
22 W. 52nd Street
New York, NY 10019
(212) 664-0995

Wayfarer Books
PO Box 1121
Davenport, IA 52805
(319) 355-3902

Wildcountry Books
236 South Third, #161
Montrose, CO 81401

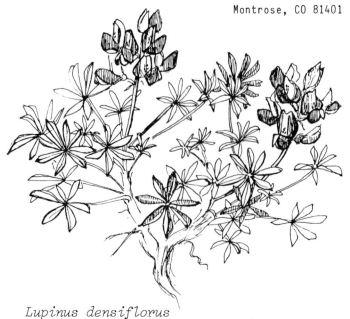

Lupinus densiflorus
Golden Gate National Recreation Area

S T A T E   A N D   P R O V I N C I A L   T O U R I S M   A G E N C I E S

ALASKA: Alaska Division of Tourism
Department of Commerce and Economic Development
Pouch E
Juneau 99811

ALBERTA: Travel Alberta
10065 Jasper Avenue
Edmonton T5J OH4

ARIZONA: Arizona Office of Tourism
3507 N. Central Avenue
Phoenix 85012

BRITISH COLUMBIA: Tourism British Columbia
1117 Wharf Street
Victoria V8W 2Z2

CALIFORNIA: California Office of Tourism
1030 13th Street, Suite 200
Sacramento 95814

COLORADO: Colorado Tourism Board
5500 S. Syracuse Circle, Suite 267
Englewood 80111

IDAHO: Idaho Tourism
State Capitol, Room 108
Boise 83720

MONTANA: Travel, Montana Department of Commerce
1424 9th Avenue
Helena 59620

NEVADA: Nevada Department of Economic Development
Capitol Complex
Carson City 89710

NEW MEXICO: Travel Division
Bataan Memorial Building
Sante Fe 87503

OREGON: Travel Information Section
595 Cottage Street NE
Salem 97310

UTAH: Utah Travel Council
Council Hall, State Capitol Hill
Salt Lake City 84114

WASHINGTON: Department of Commerce and Economic Development
Tourist Promotion Division
101 General Administration Building
Olympia 98504

WYOMING: Wyoming Travel Commission
Frank Norris Travel Center
Cheyenne 82002

THE YUKON: Tourism Yukon
Box 2745
Whitehorse Y1A 5B9

SOURCES OF MAPS

TOPOGRAPHIC MAPS

in Canada: Department of Energy, Mines and Resources
Surveys and Mappings Branch
615 Booth Street
Ottawa, Ontario K1A OE9

in the United States west of the Mississippi River including
Alaska, Louisiana and Hawaii: Branch of Distribution
United States Geological Survey
PO Box 25286
Federal Center
Denver, CO 80225

in the United States east of the Mississippi River including
Minnesota: Branch of Distribution
United States Geological Survey
1200 South Eads Street
Arlington, VA 22202

U.S. FOREST SERVICE MAPS

in Alaska: Alaska Region, USFS
PO Box 1628
Juneau, AK 99802

in Arizona and New Mexico: Southwestern Region, USFS
Federal Building
517 Gold Avenue SW
Albuquerque, NM 87102

in California: Pacific Southwest Region, USFS
630 Sansome Street
San Francisco, CA 94111

in Colorado and eastern Wyoming: Rocky Mountain Region,
USFS, 11177 W. 8th Avenue
PO Box 25127
Lakewood, CO 80225

in northern Idaho and Montana: Northern Region, USFS
Federal Building
Missoula, MT 59801

in southern Idaho, Nevada, Utah and western Wyoming:
Intermountain Region, USFS
Federal Building
324 25th Street
Ogden, UT 84401

in Oregon and Washington: Pacific Northwest Region, USFS
319 SW Pine Street
PO Box 3623
Portland, OR 97208

Stewart, British Columbia
(described under Portland Canal)